POWER SURGE
SEX, VIOLENCE & PORNOGRAPHY

POWER SURGE

SEX, VIOLENCE & PORNOGRAPHY

SUSAN G. COLE

SECOND STORY Press

CANADIAN CATALOGUING IN PUBLICATION DATA

Cole, Susan G., 1952–
Power surge

ISBN 0-929005-78-3

1. Sex. 2. Pornography. 3. Violence.
4. Women – Crimes against. I. Title.

HQ471.C65 1995   363.4'7   C95-932107-1

Edited by Beth McAuley
Cover illustration by Laurie Lafrance

Printed and bound in Canada

*Second Story Press gratefully acknowledges the assistance of
the Ontario Arts Council and The Canada Council*

SECOND STORY PRESS
720 Bathurst Street Suite 301
Toronto, Ontario
M5S 2R4

CONTENTS

Acknowledgements *7*
Introduction *9*

I SEXUALITY

What Do We Want and Why Do We Want It?
23
Making Sense of Madonna
30
Sexuality and Its Discontents
37

II PORNOGRAPHY

Confronting Pornography
53
Radical and Right Wing — There's a Difference
65
Combatting the Practice of Pornography
74
Sensationalizing Censorship
94
Kids as the Object of Art
103

III Prostitution

Sex Workers Wonder
111

Whispering Out Loud
121

Womb for Rent
126

IV Media, Culture and Sex

Unmasking the Media
141

Femme Hy Hits New Low
150

Abusive Amusement
157

Losing It on Lesbian Chic
163

V Violence

Home Sweet Home?
169

Women and Children Last
185

Sexualizing Violence
215

Feeling the Pinch on Harassment
227

Incest: Conflicting Interests
230

ACKNOWLEDGEMENTS

With a few exceptions, notably *NOW* magazine in Toronto, these pieces were published in feminist books and magazines. The great majority are taken from *Broadside*, a feminist monthly review, that published from 1978 to 1989. The articles articulate the feminist anlayses we developed as we were in the process of engaging in hands-on political action. The act of publishing was just one of these political acts. *Broadside* was published through the strength of a committed collective that devoted two nights a week and one weekend a month for ten years to producing the paper. Print fuelled the politics that fuelled the print. Without *Broadside*, and other feminist magazines like it, there would not be a movement to end violence against women. Thanks to *Broadside* collective members everywhere, especially Philinda Masters, who did the hands-on editing of the original *Broadside* pieces.

Thanks to Kristen Ruppert for unearthing the original material and to Louise Azzarello who revived it and got it into working order. Thanks also to *NOW* magazine for patience and resources, especially to computer wizards Eric Siegerman and Rick Salamat. The Metro Action Committee on Public Violence against Women and Children (METRAC) and the Barbra Schlifer Clinic in Toronto offered research resources that were indispensable in helping me update the data. Over the years many friends have influenced and encouraged me. Thanks especially this time to Darlene Lawson, who introduced me to the idea that two things can be true at the same time, and to Billee Laskin for her wisdom and openness, to my editor Beth McAuley who helped shape *Power Surge* and kept me clear and consistent, to my partner Leslie for her intense and brilliant light and to our bright, strong daughter Molly, my constant reminder of the hugeness of what's at stake.

— S.G.C.

INTRODUCTION

LONG-TIME FEMINISTS are in a serious funk. They worry about young women and their continued resistance to feminist ideas. They worry that decades of thought and activism are being lost on an X-centric generation of desensitized cyber-freaks.

I am not so worried. Women in their twenties are emerging into a world quite different from the world we encountered when feminism grew up in the late sixties. To many young women the word feminism is not charged with a sense of newness and excitement the way it was twenty-five years ago. They don't experience feminist ideas as a fresh body of breakthrough cosmic concepts that reverberate wildly through their consciousness. They don't relate to feminist thought as something they need in the way we needed it twenty-five years ago. Let's be glad of that. We helped create an environment in which women coming into their twenties already have some confidence in their own empowerment and in their ability to make an imprint on the world. You can see it in their music — from Riot Grrrls to Melissa Etheridge to Courtney Love. You can see it in their intense desire for personalized sexual expression. The title of this book, *Power Surge*, reflects the energy that is generated when women regain sexual power and expression.

I'm growing more and more convinced that a good deal of the new resistance to feminism has to do with the fact that feminist ideas are being filtered to younger women through high-profile critics of feminism who are not delivering the straight goods. When I think of young women being introduced to feminism by the likes of Christina Hoff Sommers (*Who Stole Feminism*, New York: Simon & Schuster, 1995) or Katie Roiphe (*The Morning After*, New York: Little, Brown and Co., 1993) or Camille Paglia (especially *Vamps And Tramps*, New York: Vintage, 1994) — let's call them neo-feminists — that's when I start worrying. Each of these writers is bent on portraying feminism, and especially what's been labelled radical feminism, as a point of view that casts women in the role of losers and consigns women to victim status forever. It's feminists that keep women down, not the forces of male power, they claim. And though not everyone will go as far as Paglia to say that if male power exists, women should get into it, more and more women are beginning to express the view that since male power exists and boys will be boys, girls better get used to it.

When I hear this, I feel like I'm going back in time. I watched the Clarence Thomas senate confirmation hearings with three women and one man, all over thirty years older than me, and it was a fascinating experience. When the lone man left the room, the women began to shake their heads. They did not understand the problem, not because they didn't believe Hill — they did absolutely. In fact, as often happens in these situations, the women had their own stories to tell, which they did, at first only when their male friend was out of the room, but then even when he was there. These were stories of being bugged by bosses and other male management, at the women's desks or in their offices. All of them described physical assaults of some kind. One woman began by saying that nothing like it had ever happened to her. But the women had known each other for over fifty years — they were able to help each other to remember.

The overall effect of the actual experiences turned out to be overwhelming. Their collective conclusion: 'It's part of being a working girl.' Their shared stories wound up establishing and reinforcing their certainty that sexual harassment is an everyday male behaviour to be avoided if possible and tolerated, if not. There was nothing in their experience to tell them anything other than, 'That's the way it is.' *Power Surge* is built on the principle that it doesn't have to be that way any more.

I say that despite the painful fact that, though we can point to barriers coming down over the past two decades for women in areas of employment, education and politics, and though we watch as a young generation of women grows into a world in which they can imagine their own empowerment, one thing hasn't changed very much at all: violence against women continues, virtually unstopped. 'The way it is' to my seventy-year-old friends is the way it always has been — women working, women walking, women trying to get on with their everyday lives in their homes, women everywhere having to keep that extra eye out for whoever might harm them. It used to be that we worried about strangers. Now we have to watch out for our friends. How do we know if the guy we're dating for the first time is safe? Does he give us a sign? A chance? And, of course, with close to one in four young girls having her first sexual experience at the hands of a member of her family or someone close to it, there are no guarantees of security when it comes to the family, either.

The effects are debilitating and devastating. Sexual abuse and pornography that promotes violence against women construct a sexual culture based on sexual values of dominance and submission, values we learn in our bodies, that keep men on top and women on the bottom. As it is, there isn't a word in the English language to convey a powerful and mature female sexuality. I can't imagine real sexual freedom without trying to change these conditions.

Of course, where my elderly friends' response to Anita Hill's dilemma was that she had to learn to pay the sexual price of going to work, the new neo-feminists say she should have told him to stop a few more times. She should have left her job rather than put up with it. To the date rape victims, they say, 'Learn some basic survival tactics.' This book explores why these answers are too simple and how most of the time, when women tell men to stop, they don't. It explains why this is not women's fault and documents the feminist struggle to uncover violence against women and the fight for women's bodily integrity.

It does so by going back to works written over the last fifteen years. At first I was a bit uncomfortable with the idea of going back to old work, for the usual reasons. I worried about reproducing ideas I no longer believed in. I worried that the ideas themselves might not hold. I worried that it would all look very young. I was right about the last part. Some of my early suggestions for regulating pornography are a tad naive. But there is a rawness to the expression that isn't cynical and recalls that exhilarating time when feminist ideas were simmering within the women's community and heating up the waters flowing everywhere in the mainstream. If these ideas are difficult, outrageous, if they get too close to home when it comes to sex issues, all the better. At least they come from an authentic point of passion and are not tarted up by the personality politics of those who call themselves feminist for the sole purpose of trashing basic feminist ideals and making it to the cover of *People* magazine.

Looking back I see that much of the material, though, is narrow by virtue of who I am — white, Jewish, Canadian — someone whose experience and education has been based in white Western culture. This book does not offer a global perspective. It does not embrace issues of race. It is not as layered a text as feminism itself has become. Rather, it is a record of a body of work designed to capture the early inklings that women — across lines of race, culture and class — have one thing in common: they experience violence or the threat of violence or both as a form of social and sexual control.

Power Surge is built on the principle that sex is political and begins with a section on sexuality. The piece on Madonna has a spot upfront because it encompasses ideas that resonate throughout the book — that there's more to be learned by listening than judging, that two things can be true at the same time, in this case that Madonna has power but has also been victimized, and that the way sex is presented matters deeply. "Making Sense of Madonna" also analyzes this pop icon in a way that opens a window for readers to the ideas in the following piece, "Sexuality and Its Discontents." This piece sets out a radical approach to sexuality called sex-critical.

The sections on pornography and prostitution trace the ways feminist analyses cut through the old battle lines. Before feminists started talking about pornography, the debates took place between the forces of repression, usually represented by male church leaders, and the forces of expression, usually represented by the growing breed of mainstream pornographers like Hugh Hefner — all of whom were arguing about the rights of men to masturbate to sexually explicit materials. Left out of the discussion were the women in the pictures and the women living with the consumers of pornography who felt the effect the presence of pornography was having on their lives. As pornographers defended their *expression* and the decency contingent fought for *repression*, women began to notice that whichever side won the day, it would spell *oppression* for us.

I became interested in the pornography issue when the movie *Snuff* — a film that advertises a woman's actual death as a sexual spectacle — came to town. So the early focus of my attention was on the women in pornography. It was no longer enough to wonder what effects the materials were having on the consumers. It seemed almost trivial to worry about offending somebody's morals or sensibilities. By doing so, we were missing an essential element of the female experience with pornography — what happens to the women in it. Who are they? How did they get there? The story of Linda Marchiano — once Linda Lovelace — and the brutal conditions she endured as the star of *Deep Throat* became a cautionary tale. It reminds us that the camera often disguises the force and coercion that goes into the making of pornography and ignores completely the limited choices that lead women into the production of pornography in the first place.

As I write this, the power of pornography is being conveyed daily via the sensational trial of Paul Bernardo. Bernardo is charged on multiple counts of forced confinement and the murder of two teenagers, Kristen French and Leslie Mahaffey. Central to the prosecution's case is a series of excruciatingly graphic videotapes taken by Bernardo himself as he — and his accomplice, Karla Homolka, who eventually made a deal with the crown and testified against him — sexually abused and tortured his victims. Though the tapes have not been shown publicly — much to the dismay of the CBC and other media interests — the dailies, based on the audio made available, report in devastating detail the contents of these videotapes. Like Linda Marchiano, who bravely faced talk-show audiences after she released her memoir *Ordeal*, Karla Homolka's credibility in court was severely damaged by the simple fact that she was smiling for the camera. The crimes, the disturbing relationship between Bernardo and Homolka, the fact that Bernardo felt compelled to tape everything and the way in which Homolka, a victim herself, could be made to look like she enjoyed every minute of the abuse, reveal in very specific ways the extreme example of how making pornography and getting off on it is a practice of sexual subordination.

Why did Bernardo tape his crimes? What was so important about having the record? Like former US president Richard Nixon, who taped his every consultation and abuse of power, and like senator Robert Packwood, who recorded in his diaries details of how he sexually harassed the women around him, Bernardo needed the documentation. He wanted to review it again and again. Replaying the tapes kept him blissed out on the power he held over his victims. I look at Bernardo's whole process of recording, looking and getting off sexually on what he saw and what he did as pornography. So central was this process to satisfying his power needs that, like Packwood and Nixon, the thought never crossed Bernardo's mind until it was too late that what was turning him on would ultimately turn him in.

The sections on pornography and prostitution attempt to describe the controversies that began brewing within feminism, inside artists' communities and among sex workers once we put pornography, prostitution and sex on the agenda. Women organizing against pornography had a strong impact, especially in Canada, where the courts have responded very specifically to arguments suggesting that when sexually explicit materials come under legal scrutiny, women should count for something. Recent obscenity cases reviewed in the pornography chapter take into account the possible harm to women. To be sure, censorship has been handled clumsily at times and definitely in a discriminatory way when it comes to gay and lesbian material — I favour a civil remedies appoach for reasons reviewed in this chapter. But, as I point out, Canada's censorship 'crisis' has been inflated by opportunistic writers and journalists, especially in the United States.

The litany of real abuses women experience paints a very grim picture. Taken together, the percentage of women who will experience some form of sexual abuse — battery, sexual assault, attempted sexual assault, sexual harassment — is a full 92 percent. When we look at its prevalence and the powerful system that is in place to make sure that it continues, it is very easy to get discouraged. The section on media, culture and sex suggests some teaching strategies and provides some analytical tools to deconstruct this system. These strategies offer a ray of hope. Censorship is ultimately a reactive strategy. Education is pro-active, especially educating young people early and effectively about violence against women and what to do when it touches them. The idea of incorporating studies of sexuality and violence into media education is a strategy for eliminating the market for pornography. Using pop culture artifacts as the focus invites kids into a process of change. I've found in my own teaching that finger-pointing lectures about sexual materials can only get you so far. Much better to quote Courtney Love, whose cry, "Kill girls. Watch," tells students how pornographic culture operates in a language they'll understand and a format — whether CD or video — that they can tune into.

The last section is an overview of violence against women, the radical feminist strategies developed since the seventies to fight the different abuses and how they can be applied in the nineties. The centrepiece of this section is "Sexualizing Violence," an essay that questions some basic assumptions about how these issues have been framed in the public arena. Specifically, activists in the area of violence against women have tended to separate the issues of violence and sexuality. Historically, for example, feminists have said that rape is about power, not sex. But as long as abusers come when they abuse, as long as sexual abuse survivors live with sexual confusion, the insistence on distancing sex from the issues of power looks more and more like out-and-out denial. The truth is that sexual terror — so prevalent as the data shows — plays an important role in shaping female sexuality.

As Paul Bernardo's trial has proceeded, and especially as his lawyers have cross-examined the crown's star witness Karla Homolka, Homolka has been made to look like the bad girl who desired the vicious three-way sex play that Bernardo devised. The pornography of the situation has played an important role here. But the ease with which Karla Homolka has been demonized testifies to the extent to which the public continues to be wholly ignorant of how trauma works, especially when it is sexual. Through their four-year relationship Homolka says she was beaten, coerced into sexual acts and forced to participate in the killings, including the first, and accidental, death of her own sister.

Like many battered wives, she had many opportunities to escape but did not, out of a fear. Many assaulted women stay because their husbands threaten to kill them. Once Bernardo's sexual assaults escalated to murder, Homolka had every reason to believe that he would make good on his threat. Like many incest survivors, she protected the perpetrator, took care of him, thought their relationship special and smiled for the camera the way so many assaulted daughters smile for family photos while their fathers have their arm around them.

But Homolka went farther than most. She was not just immobilized, she did not just stand paralyzed the way some mothers do when their children are abused — she actively participated in the crime. She went in the car with Bernardo while he stalked his prey. She may even have picked out some of the victims for him. She helped rape them. She often held the video camera. The extremes to which she went to serve Bernardo reflect the extremes of his sexual terrorism.

Make no mistake, I think Homolka should be held responsible for her actions — she should be in jail. But in no way is she as culpable as Bernardo. She was seventeen when they met. He was twenty-two and a seasoned rapist. And she had never hurt anybody. Patty Hearst would not have become an armed bank robber had she not been imprisoned in a closet for six days. Holocaust survivors report heartwrenchingly degrading acts — against themselves and others — undertaken to get through the experience of the concentration camps. In safety we have the luxury of seeing that Homolka had a choice to serve women up to her abuser or not. But the way Homolka was living it, the choice was between her or them.

Crucially, lawyers for Bernardo are trying to make it look like Homolka enjoyed the abuse. She has steadfastly insisted that she did not and, typically, feminist advocates would support her claim. Though "Sexualizing Violence" does not refer to Homolka specifically, it does pose the question, 'What if she did get sexual pleasure?' Would this make her any less a victim? We need to look closely at the way rape culture and rape experience define sexual experience. In court, Homolka told the story of her slow descent into sadism, the incremental steps taken in a sexual relationship that grew more and more bizarre. This is how a sexual terrorist operates. The relationship starts happily, then it turns. He makes the victim do one thing, then another, then another, then another — and then he makes her like it. That is when she is wholly subordinated and his completely.

What's interesting in all this is that most people assume that if the victim has an orgasm from the abuse, she got something out of it. The truth is that once abuse feels good, the victim did not get something, she has become nothing — which is exactly what the perpetrator wants.

The rest of the section contains essays on the different forms of sexual abuse. Taken together, the reports on sexual violence of all kinds are achingly similar. We are not ending violence against women, we are barely even regulating it. The depressing data tell the tale. We measure progress in that twenty-five years ago no one was breathing the words *rape, wife assault, sexual harassment* and *incest* and now we have built our own feminist institutions, our crisis centres and our shelters. In the past twenty-five years the services available to the survivors of violence have multiplied dramatically. This has made a difference. You can tell by the vicious backlash, especially the segment made up of abusers organizing for their right to abuse. I'm talking about fathers' rights groups all over North America and especially the manipulative minds behind the False Memory Syndrome Foundation.

The analyses in *Power Surge* are based on the radical research tool of believing women and what they say. We would know nothing about the depth of society's sexual abuse crisis were it not for the women who took — and continue to take — that courageous step of saying, 'Yes, this happened to me.' They did it and they continue to do it in the face of social forces that are thousands of years old, that are reinforced in every social institution and that appropriate new technologies for keeping women in our place. These women are speaking out against male power. That's the freedom of speech I'm fighting for.

Indeed, the movement to end violence against women has been undertaken almost entirely by women. Women created the safe environments where survivors could first share their experiences of battery, rape, sexual abuse and harassment. We have remained insistent that shelters be maintained as women-only spaces. We have undertaken to educate entire communities, most of them hostile. I believe in the autonomous women's movement and that once generated, uncorked or freed in whatever way, women's political energy is unstoppable. But — and this is another resonating theme in *Power Surge* — all this basically amounts to a mop-up operation and it has, for all intents and purposes, remained such for the past twenty-five years. And it will probably remain so if we do not engage the other 48 percent of the population in the process of change: men.

Power Surge describes how rape culture feeds male privilege and reinforces male sexual expectations of dominance and control. I say men can do something about it. They can start by respecting women's space, by doing something supportive — hot drinks after Take Back the Night marches, say — and by talking to other men about why men hurt women. And they might start to understand, for example, that it really isn't a lot to ask that they think twice before they say whatever sexual things are on their minds, whether at work or not.

Believing women and what they say is not just a good research method, it can be applied to everyday life by both men and women. Imagine you're at the office water cooler and you run into a female co-worker. You say to her, "Nice sweater you have on." She says, "I'd appreciate it if you didn't comment on my physical appearance." You just wanted to be nice and you think that her reaction is a little extreme. Fair enough. But, you have a choice of reacting to the situation in two ways. You can snort at her and tell her she's crazy. Or you can say, "Alright, thanks for telling me." The first response insists on your right to make her feel uncomfortable regardless of what she feels, the other respects whatever reasons she has for feeling the way she does. The next time you meet her at the water cooler you could make another personal comment. But you had your chance to speak, she told you how she felt — this is no silenced victim, she's speaking with clarity — and you repeated the behaviour. When you do that, it's harassment.

Finally I want to say this. It is no coincidence that the new tide of anti-feminist writing calling itself feminist comes at a time when society is having to face the fact that well over 50 percent of violence against women takes place at the hands of the men we know. It brings things down to everyday experience, how we live our lives, how we manage with co-workers, how we love our lovers. That's hard to take. It makes things very personal.

Personally, I'm not into victimization. I just keep thinking that you can't change something that you can't describe — or even face — especially if it's in your own bedroom.

SUSAN G. COLE
Toronto
July 1995

I

SEXUALITY

WHAT DO WE WANT AND WHY DO WE WANT IT?

The following represents the presentation given at the October 1, 1993 panel discussion sponsored by Media Watch and Harbourfront Centre in Toronto, Ontario.

WHILE WE THINK about and imagine about what sexuality can be and how we can all be empowered through sexuality, I ask you to keep in mind and never to close your eyes and ears to the fact that women in life can get hurt through sexuality.

I started my exploration of pornography the hard way. When the anti-pornography movement took flight fifteen years ago, it was to protest the movie *Snuff. Snuff* is absolutely the ultimate though not the typical pornographic nightmare, featuring the actual death of a woman for the sexual pleasure of the consumer.

When I first encountered *Snuff,* I began to think about pornography, but not in the old ways we used to talk about it, about how it affects the people who are using it. I wanted to start asking questions about what was going on with women who were actually in these materials. And when I talked to women who had been in pornography, I heard a lot of stories about women getting hurt. I heard stories from

Originally published as "Politics of Desire: Pornography, Erotica, Freedom of Expression" in *Fireweed,* Winter 1994.

women who were in violent pornography who said, "What you see on the page is what happened to me."

I heard these stories across the spectrum of all forms of pornography, from *Snuff* to the mainstream pornography of *Playboy* and *Penthouse*. I heard women talk to me about how they had to smile for the cameras but that didn't mean that they liked it. I heard women talk about how the pornography industry was built on the backs of sex workers. I heard women tell me that pornography was actually a better gig for them than tricking on the street. I heard women talking to me about how they posed for pictures in *Playboy* until it hurt.

When I looked at the narratives inside these sexually explicit materials, from *Snuff* to *Playboy* and *Penthouse*, I did not find what so many people craved — this extraordinary diversity and this polymorphous sexuality. I heard, rather, a series of values that consistently left the same message: 'no' means 'yes' when it comes to having sex with women; women will have sex any time, any place; women do like sex with strangers, preferably more than one stranger if she possibly encounters them.

These kinds of narratives, couched in a language of sexuality that is violent and usually degrading, I believe, are playing a very specific role in shaping the sexual values of our culture, particularly since pornography so hopelessly dominates the cultural conversation about sexuality. Given the pathetic state of sex education and given the invisibility of any kind of alternative, and given the fact that studies show that boys between the ages of fifteen and eighteen are the major market for these kinds of materials, I can begin to see these narratives and situations feeding into a rape culture, creating a generation of male sexual predators, and now that women are getting more into it, a generation of women getting off on sexual submission.

It's a system of sexuality in which I believe women lose and men lose, too. And, what's even more upsetting and frustrating, is that it almost seems to be a perfect system of sexuality, reinventing itself, teaching a kind of sexuality that actually does begin to look like it's the norm.

But who wants to live in a perfect system of sexual oppression? I don't. I want to find the way to empowerment. I desire it as much as anyone does and I think feminism is as much about empowerment as it is about facing up to women's victimization.

Still, I have the feeling, that in this culture, the act of getting up on stage and taking our clothes off or being sexual makes us more vulnerable than powerful.

That doesn't mean that we shouldn't try and that doesn't mean that I'm not speechless with admiration whenever I experience it work, whenever it actually empowers. Think about how rarely you see it happen. In mainstream culture, the examples are few: Mae West, who, by the way, never made a movie before the age of forty; Bette Midler, maybe; k.d. lang, okay; Madonna, occasionally; or think of Sandra Bernhard (though she's not exactly Ms. Mainstream). At the end of her video, *Without You I'm Nothing*, she takes her clothes off and dances with the American flag. I watch her and I can't believe that she makes it work. How does she do it?

So let's imagine being sexual as part of cultural life. We should be trying. Especially as a lesbian, I feel that way.

When you look at pornography there isn't much lesbian stuff there, except fodder for some heterosexual male fantasy. And when I look at the alternative material made by lesbians for lesbians, I ask the same questions: Who are those women? How did they get there? What's their relationship to the process? How much money are they making? Do they really choose to be there? That's what I want to know.

I set out to write a sex scene, which I'm sure amazed everybody, for my play, *A Fertile Imagination*. The play is about a lesbian couple preparing for motherhood, dealing with pregnancy in their relationship and in the world. I wanted to make it kind of a test for me. I wanted to see whether we could present some kind of visible sexuality and still keep the choice factor open. I started by thinking, 'These are my words, my sexual directions, and I leave it to the actors to perform them, so maybe that's problematic.'

But the actors were fine with it; they said, "You do your job, we'll do our job." Great. Then they whipped off their shirts. So I'm looking around, thinking, 'Oh gee, now we all have to whip off our shirts, right?' But I didn't. And that was okay with the actors, too. Now that I think of it, from the start, they couldn't wait to whip off their shirts and were, in fact, totally into it and couldn't wait to get to the sex scenes.

It turned out that in the process of doing this piece, I felt that the people in it were in control of their situation. And, ultimately, it was a real pleasure to sit in the audience and watch people react to something rarely seen on stage — women loving women.

That doesn't mean you can always control those circumstances. It's a huge risk every time out. I did get calls from people who felt uncomfortable because there were men in the audience getting off on that scene. And I did get a call from someone who said specifically that a man had been masturbating during the performance. That got me angry, because I did not create what I created so that would happen.

I would still say that I was glad that I tried to present lesbian sex, regardless of these consequences.

But I find that, with this craving for sexual empowerment, we're starting to close ourselves to another kind of reality. No matter how many times you finally have that experience of feeling that somebody's being sexually empowered, or of sexually expressing yourself and feeling that you're empowered, no matter how many times you clutch the cover of *Vanity Fair* (the November 1993 cover shows Cindy Crawford in the role of barber giving a shave to k.d. lang) to your breast and say, "This is a great thing," which I don't necessarily, but many people did, you can't close your eyes when women are getting hurt.

It's much more fun to think about getting off sexually. It's not fun to look at women's pain! I could see it happening with the sexual harassment case concerning an Ontario judge (see "Feeling the Pinch on Sexual Harassment" in section 5). I did an interview with *CBC Prime Time* and sat in front of a camera with two intelligent, professional newswomen while we reviewed the videotapes of two women giving their testimony about what had happened to them. We listened and watched while those women cried about being humiliated by the kissing judge. And when I looked at CBC's head anchorwoman and her other guest, I could feel their physical revulsion at having to watch these women's pain.

'If only the complainants had kicked him in the shins,' you hear such people say; if only they had gone to his superiors; if only they had told him to fuck off and die; if only they had gotten together as a collective of women to face him down; if only they would not cry that way. And I want to holler — if only people would stop hurting women.

Now, I don't think that censorship necessarily ends violence against women. And I especially have had problems with the use of the Criminal Code to do anything about pornography. I have had problems with giving more power to the cops and I don't think they would know pornography, or harm, if it stared them in the face. I personally favour a civil remedy that puts the power in women's hands to express what's happened to them in pornography and to sue pornographers if women have been damaged in the making, or to sue them if they've been hurt in the consumption of it, because I have heard those stories, too: I have heard how pornography has been used against women. It happens and I have the data. Now, how do we stop it from happening?

That brings me to the *Butler* decision, and I have just a few words to say about it. The old obscenity law which depended on a community standard, absolutely guaranteed that gays and lesbians were going to be targeted because we live in a homophobic culture. In a homophobic culture, if you apply a community standard, lesbian and gay materials are going to be targeted. And they have been. There are a disproportionate number of cases being brought against gay and lesbian materials and, in fact, you'd be interested to know that *Penthouse* magazine was never targeted by obscenity laws until it produced a lesbian spread in 1969. That's the one that vexed the authorities. I feel that *Butler* is a step forward in at least not targeting gay and lesbian material and in at least not targeting all sexually explicit material, and in identifying a truth that many women know and of which many women speak, which is that women are harmed in the making of pornography and in its consumption. That is why I define pornography as the sexual subordination of women in words or in pictures.

Now, I want to close by saying this hard thing. When the bust came of *Bad Attitude* (an American lesbian sex magazine), using the *Butler* decision, I was completely appalled, I was so upset. Of all the things to go after, does it have to be lesbian material? But I have to say, despite my associate's comments before me, that when I looked at the materials, I did see women hurting each other. And when I was asked whether I would go out on a demonstration to protest the bust, I said I would say on paper that I think it is a bad thing to discriminate against gay and lesbian material, but that I could not go on the line on that one. I cannot give the smallest message that I think it's okay for women to hurt each other. I'm not saying that a cop should go in and stop you, or that any guardian should go in and stop you. I'm certainly not going to stop you. I just don't want to participate in it. That isn't the world I'm trying to build. That isn't the world I'm fighting for.

I am not fighting for the world where women can sexually express themselves by experiencing pain. In my vision, women and men don't feel so cut off from our bodies that we torture our genitalia so that we can feel something. I want to end violence against women and build a healed community. And that's what I'm engaging you in as well.

MAKING SENSE OF MADONNA

Through the eighties and the nineties, Madonna has been the most talked about woman in North America. Her growing influence over pop culture has always been a source of dismay for women who aspire to more of a personal identity than sex object, boy toy or sexploitation queen. But not me. Frankly, I liked her from the start. My responses grew more complicated as she changed from the brash, chubby, twenty-year-old to the sleek thirty-something power broker. But, regardless of what she does, her personal and professional life remain a public testing ground for sexual attitudes.

I WENT TO Exhibition Stadium last night to see Madonna in concert and when it was over I felt that I had seen a variation on the theme of female empowerment.

Madonna? Female empowerment? Have I lost my mind? I am aware that feminists do not constitute the grassroots of the Madonna fan club. Madonna is and does a lot that drives feminists crazy. She presents herself as a boy toy and that's trouble, for women and for young women in particular. She abuses sex and uses it to give the impression that it's perfectly all right to kick and claw and sleep your way to the top. That's also trouble for young women who may not know that most women who try to climb the ladder through sex wind

---

Part of the following article was published as "Balls and Boy Toys" in *Broadside*, August/September 1987.

up on the bottom, not the top. Her songs, taken together, reveal a retro politic, in particular her recent hit, "Papa Don't Preach," which celebrates a pregnant teenager's decision to keep her baby — the teenager is anti-choice. Her latest image makeover as Marilyn Monroe only further constructs her as sex object and aggrandizes her as pop icon, possibly at the expense of a woman seriously victimized. She married bad-boy punch-out artist Sean Penn. This, you can hear women-positive women say, is not good for women.

Why doesn't a reasonable, woman-positive type like myself buy all of this? Let me start at the beginning of my own process. I first got interested in Madonna when I saw her in a film called *Desperately Seeking Susan*, a wonderful movie, written, directed and produced by women (Susan Seidelman is the film's creative force), about a suburban housewife's attempt to overcome her ennui. I thought Madonna's presence in this subversive film said a great deal about what mattered to her.

I rented the video of Madonna's first live tour. I saw a young, vulnerable, aggressive, wildly talented woman who was completely sure of what she wanted. She didn't look anything like a boy toy, and if she were one, she struck me as the kind that would blow up in somebody's face. By the way, she kept her clothes on throughout the performance.

She wasn't a boy toy then, and if her recent performance is any indication, she is definitely not a boy toy now. She's more interested in the Marilyn Monroe connection and has dyed her hair blonde to evoke the former screen legend. Some of you who are aware that Marilyn Monroe was made over as a boy toy for all of Hollywood may not measure progress here. But I think Madonna wants to bring Monroe back to the eighties for a reason. Think of what Monroe and Madonna have in common. Both of them were forced to model nude early in their careers. Both of them realized that sex was the enforced rate of exchange in the entertainment business. They never used sex as a replacement for work, they used sex to have a chance to work. But Marilyn Monroe is dead and Madonna is alive as the most powerful woman in pop music today. I can do what she did, says Madonna, but I'm sticking around.

I think it's wrong to say that Madonna abuses sex. I think Madonna has been abused in sex and I call her a survivor. When Bob Guccione published nude photographs of former Miss America Vanessa Williams without her consent, he did it to humiliate her, to take away from her everything she might have gained. (Williams disappeared for a decade but emerged in the early nineties as a pop singer of note.) He (and competitor *Playboy*) published nude photographs of Madonna without her consent for the same reason. The message was, 'You think you're making it. Try it. I will always reduce you to what you had to do to survive.'

But Madonna didn't go away. I like that about her. I like the fact that she did not let pornographers take her voice away. As for her body, it is not just a sex machine for the audience. She can dance, something for which critics haven't given her much credit, and her performance carries with it her own personal message. At this point, I think she comes closer to having performed the political miracle of sexual empowerment (on and off stage — she's filed for divorce from Sean Penn) than most female performers.

Many friends of mine complain about the anti-choice sentiment of "Papa Don't Preach." But this furor over the song makes me think that our abortion politics have become really flabby. The song tells the story of a teenage woman who wants to keep her child. What's wrong with that? I thought we were for choice. Since when we do we assume that teenage women shouldn't have the choice to bear children? Do we think abortion is better? Do we think having the child and giving it up to an adoption agency is better? Or easier?

It intrigues me that the feminist controversy over this song focuses on whether she chooses abortion rather than on her need to justify everything to Papa in the first place. Madonna, a proud product of Catholic repression (who wears crucifixes, she says, because they have naked men on them) understands the essence of hierarchy and control, and she understands whom women have to answer to when they get in trouble.

At the end of her concert version of "Papa Don't Preach," a mammoth slide reading SAFE SEX stares out at the audience. I don't know anyone else who would have included such a blatant message outside an AIDS benefit context. When you think that television networks won't advertise condoms in the most indirect and inoffensive ways, you have to hand it to Madonna for bravery and for having taken the responsibility when our other institutions have abdicated theirs. Her last words, before Goodnight, were, "That's right folks, use condoms."

She's ahead of her time, I'd say.

Update 1995

THE POP TART everyone was laughing at ten years ago has generated tons of ink by now and there's surely some poetic justice in the fact that academics have embraced Madonna as a worthy thesis topic. But not a word of it has satisfied my own gnawing suspicions.

I'm one of those who has felt deep conflict about this extraordinary woman. I've admired her safe sex stance, taken as early as 1986, when she turned a live version of "Papa Don't Preach" into a lesson in safe sex and hosted a ground breaking AIDS benefit at Madison Square Gardens. I knew

---

Parts of this update were originally published as "Making Sense of Madonna" in *Herizons*, Spring 1993.

enough to know that choosing sexuality as a means to power is not exactly a new female strategy. In fact, it has been the only strategy available to women for many years in many cultures. But there was something fresh about her. She had bad taste — something I admire in high-profile women — and didn't care, and she had a street smart thing that was brash and appealing.

But I've just seen the cover of November's *Vanity Fair* — Madonna as a pigtailed child, naked in water wings. My first thought was not, 'How could she?' I could only think, 'Something happened to her. What was it?' Indeed, it strengthened my sense that Madonna's sexual ferocity always seemed so radical, precisely because it was mixed with the desperation of a true survivor. I've harboured suspicions for some time — I have a clipping collection to show for it — but I couldn't satisfy my ethical qualms about claiming to know someone else's story, and having the arrogance to write about it.

But I'm growing impatient looking at her *Sex* book and I want to tell it like I see it.

"Generally," she writes in *Sex*, "I don't think pornography degrades women. The women who are doing it want to do it." Really? Which women is she talking about? She's taking in $5.5 million for sexually explicit photographs whose production she controlled completely. The real lives of women in the real world of pornography are not like that. "There are women in abusive relationships who are trapped," she writes, "but I have friends who have money and are educated and they stay, so they must be getting something out of it." Who's they? Maybe Madonna is one of those women. Why did Sean Penn — whom she still calls the love of her life — "patrol her wardrobe," and why did her manipulation at the hands of Warren Beatty eventually become an embarrassingly public spectacle? Why does one of the most powerful women in the entertainment business — a control freak, they call her — keep going back to controlling relationships?

Understand that it is not that she has the 'wrong line' on sex and violence that bothers me, although I think her comments are anti-woman and trivialize decades of agonizing feminist activism. What upsets me is that she has no empathy for experiences that seem to be her own. This icon, celebrated for being ultra-revealing, refuses to speak in the first person. And when she does, as in the tell-all *Truth or Dare* film documentary, the braggadocio claim that she exposes everything is pretense only. She hasn't told us yet who she really is.

Her mother died when she was six and she grew up the only female in a household with her father and five brothers. What was that like? Why is she so obsessed with her father? From "Papa Don't Preach" to "This Used to be My Playground" to the latest "Deeper and Deeper," she just can't seem to ditch him. And who is that creepy brother in *Truth or Dare*, the one who keeps disappointing the star by not showing up? When he finally does, he has five male friends in tow. "Tell him I want my privacy," she says to the camera and she slams the door.

Her videos and songs reveal quite a bit. Our first glimpse in *The Virgin Tour* video shows her giggling like a five-year-old and sexualizing herself at the same time. She made a big hit out of a song that sounded cryptic but perhaps isn't — what's the secret she wants to "Live to Tell?" Now on the *Bedtime Stories* CD, she writes, "My Baby's Got A Secret." And really, why does she say in *Truth or Dare* that her father fucked her? "Just kidding," she giggles. Why would anyone joke about this stuff?

Applying what we know about sexual abuse helps clarify a few things. There's her sexual precocity. She appears to have begun posing nude when she was a barely post-pubescent girl. (*Penthouse* and *Playboy* published such photos without her permission in 1984.) There's the pattern of being attracted to controlling men. There's her tendency to infantalize herself sexually. There's her inability to sustain a professional

connection without having sexual relationships with her col-
laborators. And out of her latest caper, the S/M-laden book,
emerges a woman who can't imagine a sexual moment without somebody getting hurt. How did this happen?

These questions go right to the heart of feminist analysis
— which comes out of women's experience. And looking for
the answers frees us from the narrow limits of the current
debate, the one that embraces that tiresome good-girl/bad-
girl dichotomy. I don't want to have to choose between
whether Madonna's sexy and therefore good for women, or
sexy and therefore bad for women. I want to know why she
does what she does.

Looking at Madonna as a survivor — of whatever —
enables us to be for her, not against her. This perspective does
not — as the pro-sex, pro-S/M contingent will be quick to
claim — dismiss her as a victim. It celebrates her strength,
her audacity in making survival her own stunning power trip
and the ultimate victory she's gained by turning sex into
something she can exploit for her own ends.

Madonna may have taken off all her clothes but she has
not yet begun to strip back the emotional layers. When she
does, when she reaches back and finds that memory, who
knows? My guess is she'll be a remarkable artist.

SEXUALITY AND ITS DISCONTENTS

Though you'd never know it from the works by high-profile critics of feminism in the nineties — and the way they have been hailed as breakthrough thinkers — feminists have been engaged in an intense debate on sexuality, victimization and power since the early eighties. Here is an essay written in response to the first rumblings of pro-sex feminism that bubbled out of grassroots feminist communities in 1984. Pro-sex feminists believe that feminists fighting violence against women tend to see women only as victims in sex and that free sexual expression and exploration are central to women's liberation. The following article makes the point that there is no free sexuality to explore. The bibliography has not been updated as I think these groundbreaking feminist works should be acknowledged.

I

In sex, what works, what brings mutual pleasure should be the criterion of "good." The problematic issue is consent, not whether my desire is better than yours.

— Esther Newton, Shirley Walton,
"The Misunderstanding,"
Pleasure and Danger.

Originally published in *Broadside*, April 1988.

WITH A FEW exceptions here and there, most women I know would like to have more and better sex, and they wish it would last longer. Many women are relieved that feminism has finally got around to talking sex. I mean talking good sex. Good sex, not the frightening kind that Ti-Grace Atkinson was writing about in her radical essay "The Institution of Sexual Intercourse" (in *Notes From the Second Wave*, 1972). Atkinson argued that since sexual intercourse was good only for male pleasure (the myth of the vaginal orgasm had just been exposed) and for getting women pregnant, the 'act' itself was patriarchal to the core. Good sex, not the protestations of celibates who claim that it is easier not to bother and that sex gets in the way of political action. Good sex, not the kind we hear about again and again where sex gets defined as women's sexual abuse. Good sex, the kind that feels good, the kind that empowers women, the kind that redefines sexuality in our own terms. Now really, who could be against that? After Atkinson, celibacy and the litany of sexual abuses that are real for women, feminist theorists would like to take sex back.

The catalogue of feminist literature on the subject has been beefed up considerably over the past several years by the publication of a number of books focussing on sexuality and related issues (see bibliography). The British anthology *Sex and Love* reflects a wide range of opinions, but two American books, *Powers of Desire* (especially the section on current controversies) and the more recent *Pleasure and Danger*, sustain the argument that it is crucial for feminists to stop harping on our potential for victimization in the sexual arena and necessary for us to get to the good part — the good sex, the kind where women become sexual subjects not sexual objects, where female desire is fulfilled.

Read Ellen Willis's "Feminism, Moralism and Pornography," read Judith R. Walkowitz's "Male Vice and Female Virtue," both in *Powers of Desire*. Add to that Ellen DuBois's "Seeking Ecstacy on the Battlefield: Danger and

Pleasure in Nineteenth-Century Feminist Sexual Thought" in *Pleasure and Danger* and the pattern begins to appear. These writers insist that, historically, feminism has scared women away from sex, that feminism has characterized women as the bearers of a moral standard in such a way as to make the right wing proud; and that feminism has created a theoretical framework in which there is no safe sex. We are left, they argue, with a liberation that can only come from sexual purity. To writers reared in the sixties and in a culture that gives enormous rewards for sexual appeal, the nineteenth-century feminists — and those Willis would call their imitators in the second wave — are no fun at all.

Having vilified feminists in the first wave for associating freedom with sexual abstinence, new feminist writing, as evidenced in the quote above, criticize the second-wave backlash and insist that sexual liberation equals sexual activity, period. Women have had no authentic sexual voice, you can hear the 'let's do it' women say. How can we know what we want unless we 'explore more'? Women have been allowed no sexuality. Expression is everything. Imbedded in this view is the notion that sex is proto-social, that is, untrammeled by patriarchal concerns of power and powerlessness, and that by engaging in sexual activity we can reclaim it, we can change it. Female orgasms will make us free. In a hypersexualized culture where personal identity is so wrapped up in sexuality, where sex symbol Madonna calls herself a feminist and even the women's movement has its sex symbols, this sex-positive feminism sounds very appealing. But we accept the view uncritically at our peril. To embrace it is to underestimate the extent to which sexuality is a social construct not so easily undone by female orgasms, per se.

II

To simply celebrate whatever gives us pleasure seems to me both problematic and too easy; we need to analyze how it is that certain things turn us on, how sexuality has been constructed under patriarchy to produce pleasure in the dominant submissive forms, before we advocate these modes.

— E. Ann Kaplan, "Is the Gaze Male?," *Powers of Desire.*

Like Kaplan, I think it is important for feminists to identify a patriarchal sexual ideology that is held together by three strands. The first is the practice of forced heterosexuality, a phenomenon addressed by Adrienne Rich in "Compulsory Heterosexuality and Lesbian Existence" (reprinted in *Powers of Desire*). Feminists have begun to unpack the cultural and sexual baggage with which this particular ideological strain has saddled us, and that struggle in the second wave, with the high profile of lesbian activists, has produced a lively debate that recognizes the Lavender contingent as a vital, perhaps central, force in a sexually conscious movement.

The second ideological strand perpetuates the women-as-submissive/men-as-dominant configuration within the heterosexual paradigm. Pornography's practice of eroticizing sexual subordination is particularly useful in the promulgation of dominant/submissive male/female gender categories. Pornography is just one of the cultural institutions committed to this second strain. There is a great deal else done to make our own demise sexually arousing to men: for example, some of the more excessive and sexually explicit rock videos; the dynamics of Harlequin Romances; or the increasing expression of violent chic in fashion magazines. What is crucial about the way sexual ideology works is that it does not operate on the 'idea' level. It works in our bodies. That is why pornography is more than just speech. It says something, but it is designed specifically to elicit a physical response.

Just as a great number of women think that heterosexuality is their 'natural' choice and not relentlessly promoted by a culture that needs it badly, many men and women really 'feel' aroused by domination and surrender. Mine is not an argument for feminist essentialism and the acceptance of male and female qualities as natural. If women were born to submit and men to dominate, why do the products of culture have to keep reminding us about it? The answer is — so that those products will condition us. The fact that men get to act in the world, and women get to nurture them in their pursuits, gets acted out in sexual terms as men act and women receive — sexually. Men take and women are taken. The reason why penile penetration is generally interpreted as a man invading and not as a woman engulfing is that a word like engulfing, or even the practice itself, is inconsistent with our culture's sexual ideology.

Even the most enlightened and progressive women and men get off on pornography's sexual subordination. This does not make these people sick, weird or perverted, it makes them well-socialized products of a culture determined to make sexuality the most powerful force for keeping us in our rightful places. Other forms of sexual socialization are sexual abuse and ritual abuse, which teach girls to be subordinate. What is publicly displayed in pornography happens repeatedly behind closed doors. Feminists have argued closely that pornography lies. I think we have to accept that the lie of pornography, and of the media products that share pornographic values, is becoming the truth about life. I do not think that feminists have come to grips with this second strand of patriarchal sexual ideology, at least not enough to change it.

Given the definition of sexuality under patriarchal construction, the best we've been able to do in the feminist struggle has been to fiddle ever so slightly with a few roles, give lesbians a chance to be 'tops' as well as 'bottoms,' without challenging the hierarchical construct in the first place. Actually, the very best evidence we have that sexuality is socially constructed and not biologically determined is the fact that not only have some lesbians resisted the ideology of forced heterosexuality, but have resisted the male/dominant female/submissive role demands by changing the roles in S/M scenarios at will.

The third strand of patriarchal sexual ideology is the tenet that power and sex are inextricably bound, that sex without aggression and violence and tension and conflict is non existent, or boring at best. Judging by material in the new feminist texts, this third strand is not only not rejected in the new thinking, but is actively embraced by feminists who would rather have power-laden sex than no sex at all.

Although the evidence for this abounds in both *Powers of Desire* and *Pleasure and Danger*, the capitulation to the third strand is most plainly put by Esther Newton and Shirley Walton in "The Misunderstanding" (*Pleasure and Danger*), where they explain their failure to consummate their friendship by the fact that they were incompatible: they were both tops. They don't bother to analyze how this came to be. In fact, they refuse to deal with it at all and submerge the entire question of power into a scenario where nature wants it that way. "Power and sexual desire," they write "are *deeply, perhaps intrinsically,* connected in ways we do not fully understand and just can't abolish." (Italics mine.)

Some feminists are so solidly in the grip of the sex-can-only-equal-power ideology that when I suggested a real alternative to the dynamic — i.e., a serious feminist initiative to eroticize equality in both our cultural product and in our personal sexual practice — a feminist writing for the vehemently sex-positive gay news magazine *The Body Politic* reported that I had advocated celibacy.

Newton and Walton deliver the female-orgasm-equals-radical-change motif. When they say, "What works is what's good," they mean that what works is what feels good. But what feels good is constructed from something other than a feminist framework, like thousands of years of sexual oppression and the perpetuation of a sexual ideology that is certain to keep women down. Why do so-called 'pro-sex' feminists no longer care about this, or ignore it, or misinterpret it, or reinterpret it in a desperate attempt to avoid the anti-sex 'prude' label?

Muriel Dimen, in her article "Politically Correct? Politically Incorrect?" (*Pleasure and Danger*), tries to be conciliatory but winds up saying that sex and political correctness are incompatible. "Sexual intimacy," she writes, "is resistant to rules of political correctness, or rather when it succumbs to rules, passion disappears." But Dimen has not only missed the point, she has turned it around. Feminists do not set the rules, patriarchy does. The very source of our passion is rooted in patriarchal interests. For some reason, Dimen worries more about feminists telling her what to do than the extent to which a bona fide sexual ideology has already laid down the rules for her. Given the absence of close analysis in these discussions, and at the rate some feminists are espousing the view that more sex is the answer, I'm beginning to think that even though I care about the quality of sexual life, I'll concede them the pro-sex label, the way feminists have had to concede the pro-life label to the right wing even though we know we care a great deal more about the quality of life issues. If pro-sex means the celebration of sex, the doing of it, at all costs, I'd rather be, well, pro-choice. Which is to say, I'd rather fight for a world in which consent had some real meaning.

III

Erotic chauvinism cannot be redeemed by tarting it up in Marxist drag, sophisticated constructionist theory or retro-psychobabble.

> — Gayle Rubin, "Thinking Sex,"
> *Pleasure and Danger.*

Just as agreeing not to mention danger requires that one's sexual autobiography be recast, agreeing not to speak about pleasure requires a similar dishonest alchemy, the transmutation of sexuality into unmitigated danger and unremitting victimization.

> — Carole S. Vance, "Pleasure and
> Danger: Toward a Politics of
> Sexuality," *Pleasure and Danger.*

The tendency of some feminists to regard women purely as victims rather than sexual subjects, and to define the movement's goal as controlling male sexuality rather than demanding women's freedom to lead active sexual lives, reinforces women's oppression and plays into the hands of the new right. It is a dead end, a politics of despair. Feminism is a vision of active freedom of fulfilled desires, or it is nothing.

> — Ellen Willis, *Diary of a Conference
> on Sexuality* (out of print).

Sex is not the problem, sexism is.

> — Lisa Steele, "A Capital Idea," *Women
> Against Censorship.*

These quotations are taken from among the most eloquent proponents of a new feminist perspective on sexuality. To what extent do they take on the issue of patriarchal sexual ideology? Not much, from what I can see. Gayle Rubin, whose article "Thinking Sex" is really the centrepiece of *Pleasure and Danger* (and who unfortunately repudiates the truly brilliant "Traffic in Women," which she wrote in 1973), does an exhaustive analysis of the way in which legal proscription against sexual behaviour has caused unspeakable trauma for people who have done nothing to warrant such persecution. Her critique of legal sanction is extremely useful. Rubin has always been a force to reckon with in this debate. But her main point is that erotic chauvinism is reprehensible: "Variation is a fundamental property of life ... yet sexuality is supposed to conform to a single standard." But Rubin picks on the wrong standard. She worries about the persecution of S/M practitioners and 'cross generational' sexual activists, calling them the true dissidents, when in fact they express one of the fundamental elements in patriarchal ideology — the desire to dominate.

In her introduction to *Pleasure and Danger*, Carole S. Vance complains that feminists have transmuted sexuality into unmitigated damage, once again placing the blame on feminists for theorizing about how sexuality works. Ellen Willis also wants to be a sexual actor and not a victim, as if we could wish away an ideology that is deeply entrenched. Why do these women resist the idea that sexuality is gendered to the ground? I think they resist the view because they are eager for sexual freedom and they do not believe that they can get it as long as they think of themselves as victims. To say that women are not victims in sex becomes the means for them to feel empowered in the sexual arena. While I sympathize with their desires, I don't think putting on blinkers is the answer.

To say that women are not victims in sex is to trivialize everything we know about rape, incest and wife assault (see "Sexualizing Violence" in section 5). I do not think we can afford to do that lest we retreat into the silence that has kept women victimized for so long. The desire for orgasm is not worth that. This is not to say that we shouldn't have sex. It means we have to continue to question how and why we get our pleasure; we have to question the role of sexual intercourse in a sexist culture; we have to question the social meaning of fellatio; we have to question the ways in which conflict, aggression and hierarchy get us hot. We should be able to do so without anyone thinking we are saying women should stop participating in any of these activities. This tendency to sniff out 'censors' and 'judgements' in the feminist debate permeates Gayle Rubin's article, for example. She seems to think that just talking about these things means the same thing as applying legal sanction. Free speech advocates, of all people, should know the difference between people who have opinions about sex and the sex police.

What's fascinating about the new developments is that women like Carole S. Vance and Ellen Willis are anti-censorship feminists with strong views about the action of state and legal mechanisms. Both of these women would be prepared to argue meticulously that patriarchal structures exist to maintain the status of the powerful over the powerless. The question here is this: Why is sexuality so different? Why can we agree that cultural and political life have been organized over centuries to protect the status quo — with few reforms allowed — while sexuality has not? Why does the left wing, for that matter, automatically become victim-oriented when analyzing the state, but refuse to question the way in which sexuality can be used against us? If the forces of political dominance have been so careful to appropriate every other avenue of human expression and change, and given what we know about sexuality's potential for empowerment, why and how could we imagine that the forces of political power would have left sexuality out?

The new sex-positive feminism seems to assume that the operative sexual ideology of patriarchy, if one exists, had been repression and not oppression. I am not impressed with this view. I look around in this culture and I do not see a great deal of repression. I see a hypersexualized society less concerned with having no sex, than with having the right kind of sex — men on top, women on the bottom; a society in which, for example, American men spend fifty million dollars a day on prostitution. These men spend the money to have sex, not to avoid it. This is a culture in which men's sexual access to women is guaranteed by a pornography industry that remains for all practical purposes protected, or by health workers who in the wake of wife assault, tell the victims to go home and be more feminine, or by law enforcement officers who think wife assault is 'just sex,' or that marital rape is a man's right; a culture where adolescent women purchase T-shirts with a heavy metal rock band's logo featuring women in chains on their hands and knees, and advertise their inevitable readiness to participate in sex that will sit quite nicely with patriarchal constructs; and finally, where one out of four women will have her first sexual experience before the age of sixteen with a member of her family or someone close to it, in a context of force and inequality. Likely no one will find out, and she will learn that sexuality is essentially a source of her own victimization and she'll go into the world accepting that this is the way sex is meant to be. Cultural products aren't the only things that keep us in line. Real experience works just as well.

Lisa Steele's "Capital Idea" in *Women Against Censorship* is a thorough analysis of how mass media sex stereotyping keeps the prevailing sexual ideology unthreatened. But I disagree with the comment that "sex is not the problem, sexism is," even though it is a formulation feminists, especially anti-porn feminists, have espoused since the critique was first developed. Sex is a problem for a lot of women. Ann Landers found that out and I think that is the significance of her 1985 survey. When she asked her readers whether they preferred cuddles to 'the act,' 72 percent of women preferred cuddles to the act.

I mentioned this poll to a woman who would no doubt appreciate the 'sex-positive' label. Her response was swift: 'I'm in the other 28 percent.' The implication is, 'What's wrong with the other 72 percent? Maybe if they weren't so repressed they would get into it more.' But the women who responded to Ann Lander's poll did not say they preferred the cuddles because the Bible told them that fornication was a sin; they did not complain about jism and come and how it made them gag. Their problem was not that sex was 'yucky.' Their problem was that they felt used up, as if the act were the exercise of power over them and not something which gave them pleasure. These women are resisting. What's amazing, given the intensity with which they are encouraged to like it the way it is, is that there were so many of them who were willing to say that they didn't. They deserve our support, not our contempt.

What most of us want to believe is that sexuality is unremittingly positive. We want to believe this because sex gives us pleasure, regardless of whether it has been constructed by political ideology and its cultural agents. Sometimes women can be heard arguing that they like to be sexual objects. What they mean is that they like to have sex, that they cannot imagine anything else but the objectification through sexual response.

The last time I heard a woman say this, she was cheered by an audience who agreed that she shouldn't have to give up sex. She and her audience's insistence that sexual objectification was worth maintaining, lest none of us ever has sex again, locks out change. Objectification, conflict and danger in the sexual arena are not inevitable for women.

We do not have to give up on sexual pleasure, but we cannot afford to be afraid to examine where it comes from and how we get it and what happens in the sexual arena. Why jump into the arena unprepared? We have to criticize it, analyze it and know its values.

We have to understand our victimization — face it and not deny it — as well as the conditioning that leads us to it. In the lead article in *Women Against Censorship*, Varda Burstyn warns that we have to be careful about the strategies we develop, "to mend and reweave the delicate fabric of sexual life." Sexual life does need mending and reweaving, and with an entirely new set of threads and strands.

The feminist struggle is not against sexuality, it is the struggle for change in the sexual arena.

That change can come about in many ways. Sex education that takes issues of violence against women seriously is one thing that we need. Another thing we need is imagination. For imagine how the world would look, imagine how the world would feel if we spent as much money, time and resources on eroticizing equality as we do sexualizing violence and control.

FURTHER READING

Varda Burstyn, ed. *Women Against Censorship*. Toronto and Vancouver: Douglas and McIntyre, 1985.

Sue Cartledge and Joanna Ryan, eds. *Sex and Love: New Thoughts on Old Contradictions*. London: The Women's Press, 1983.

Anne Snitow, Christin Stansell and Sharon Thompson, eds. *Powers of Desire: The Politics of Sexuality*. New York: Monthly Review Press, 1983.

Carole S. Vance, ed. *Pleasure and Danger: Exploring Female Sexuality*. Boston: Routledge and Keagan Paul, 1984.

II

PORNOGRAPHY

CONFRONTING PORNOGRAPHY

Many would say that the feminist movement against pornog-
raphy officially began when activists in Rochester, New York,
protested the screening of the movie Snuff *in 1977. Snuff was*
advertised as featuring the actual death of a woman as sexual
spectacle. I was involved in protests when Snuff *arrived in*
Toronto a year later. Eventually the commercial movie ver-
sion was revealed as a hoax, but police have linked videotapes
to sexual slayings and, now, videotapes of accused Paul
Bernardo's tortured victims figure prominently in Toronto's
most sensational trial in decades. (Bernardo is on trial for the
murders of fourteen-year-old Leslie Erin Mahaffy in 1991,
and fifteen-year-old Kristen Dawn French in 1992.)

Because Snuff *was the impetus for early actions against*
pornography, first thoughts on the subject, including my own,
focussed on violent pornography. In many ways, this was a
superficial analysis, for it didn't take into account the violence
against women that might be going on off camera in the mak-
ing of pornography. It also makes it look as if sex is not our
issue. And it makes it just that bit easier to argue in favour of
*censorship. In the post-*Snuff *environment, I went so far as to*
call myself pro-censorship. I don't anymore. But I appreciate
the way the early focus on violence helped raise the stakes in the
censorship debate as well as raise new questions as to whether
liberal values promoted social change or the status quo.

Originally published in *Broadside*, November 1981.

I

MOST OF US pretend that it isn't there. Every newsstand is jammed with it. In the back of almost every variety store entire displays are devoted to it. Partly because we can't believe that the fear and loathing of women can be so strong, we try to shut it out. The pornographic image, woman in a state of ecstasy, the plaything of her male master; woman grovelling for more abuse; woman strapped in leather, straining to get loose; woman still hungry for the next lash. Who is she? How much longer, even as we avert our gaze, can we pretend that she isn't affecting us?

Essentially we tend to exclude the pornographic image from among those that really matter because the image is perceived to be a fringe phenomenon, part of the underside of our culture. But the profit figures associated with the pornography industry, greater than those of the film and record industries combined, suggest that this is big business and not a series of fly-by-night operations designed to cater to the transient and the furtive.

And the industry is far from underground. The makers of the National Film Board's *Not a Love Story*, a film about pornography, travelled to the peep shows, the live shows and the trench-coated set to uncover horrifying images of women. But the most grotesque portrait was not to be found in the bowels of our culture. It was there on the cover of *Hustler* magazine — a woman's body churning through a meat grinder and available on every newsstand in the US.

We are expected to accept that a guy aroused to orgasm by the sight of a woman being brutalized is a relatively benign phenomenon, that we should leave the poor fellow alone in his fantasy world. And who are we anyway to deign to exercise the kind of thought control that would judge anyone's fantasies? Fantasies, after all, are an inalienable right. This would be a very useful question were it true that the male fantasizer is repulsed by his tendencies, filled with self-loathing because he needs to conjure up the image of a violated female body for a sexual object that he has been taught to love.

But *he* isn't conjuring up the hideous images. The pornographer does it for him. And the men in the films and photographs who shove bamboo up women's vaginas are not depicted as crazed weirdos. Quite the contrary, they are lionized, imbued with strange powers, role models, if you will, for the fantasizer. Whereas it could be true that a random male, may, if left to his own devices and fantasies, develop a sense that his proclivities are peculiar, that something is not quite right, the pornography presented in mass quantity serves the function it would in any mass medium. It legitimizes the consumer's disease. Far from bringing the consumer to terms with who he really is, the pornographer absolves him of his guilt.

The pornographer's strategy is to harp on the symbols already woven into our cultural fabric; particularly the dual symbol of woman as either whore or virgin. She is either destructively depraved or completely innocent until, with the invasion of one of her orifices, she finds her true self — sexually berserk. Of late, the consumer of pornography can get the best of the virgin and the whore. Women are as corrupt as ever, enjoying especially masochistic experiences that find her branded with hot irons or gang-raped. Less and less, though, is she portrayed as the coy virgin. That role now falls increasingly on the shoulders of children.

Women in pornography are totally depraved, capitulating to a sexual frenzy brought on by the manipulations of a masterful male. It is an image of women possessed, at once by her uncontrollable sexual urges and by the men who can exploit them. The very existence of the myriad photographs and films of women as victims give to the men who peer at them a sense that women are worthless. Just the fact that women pose for them is proof of our depravity. That women who work in the industry do so mostly because of a lack of economic options is no matter. That the only other option available to many women in the trade is prostitution, one they perceive to involve many more risks, is of course not going to cross the consumer's mind. According to the man getting off, if the women submit to the humiliation of being photographed or filmed, then they must also like the sexual humiliation going on in the film.

Of course fantasies are an inalienable right, provided that they remain fantasies. The rise in the rape rate and the incidence of violence against women in the home provides a convincing argument against the notion that pornography is a safety valve that keeps men off the street and without any need to act violently. We are told nevertheless that the pornographic image is harmless and that under no circumstances is it ever translated back to real women in the real world.

We have some tidbits of information that if borne in mind serve as a reminder that media images are powerful indeed.

New York: a film entitled *The Warriors* is released and frequented by patrons anxious to experience the gang warfare depicted in the film. And experience it they did. In fact, members of the audience went on a rampage of the theatre while the film was being shown. Florida: a youngster replicates a violent crime he has seen on a made-for-TV movie. California: sexual therapists accept film as an effective tool for practising sexual therapy. And everywhere in the world the advertising industry relies on the precept that the medium delivers a message, one so convincing as to move the receiver of the message to buy a product. The idea that the pornographic image has no impact appears to be but wishful thinking as it goes against one of the critical assumptions of the adman, himself part of the very backbone of our consumer society.

The pornographic image itself is not a great deal different from the one that graces countless billboards or the movie and television screens. That 'something about an Aqua Velva man' that makes women go wild is the same awesome power he has over the female in girlie magazines. The pornographer is no rebel. He reinforces values already prevalent in our culture. He is the absolver of the fantasizer's guilt as he informs his consumer that the desire to violate women is not only acceptable but has its own rewards. With the possible exception of the advertising executive, he is our culture's most effective propagandist, designing as he does this vicious hate campaign. His success depends upon our silence and our pretending that it isn't there.

II

It is not always easy to break the silence. Those of us who have made attempts to explore the issue publicly have been shocked by the hostility in the reactions to a fresh perspective on pornography. Telling it like it is makes many people uncomfortable. The women who made the NFB film *Not a Love Story* (reviewed in *Broadside*, October 1981) were baffled by the fury of male reviewers, one of whom called the movie a sample of fascist bourgeois feminism. The film critic in question, who no doubt fancies himself a progressive, was referring to what he perceived to be the film's positive stance on censorship.

What had gone wrong? The film's only statement on censorship was made by Susan Griffin and she articulated a point of view against censorship. The filmmakers themselves were confused on the subject and were inclined to shy away from the censorship solution. The film, a collage of images from the world of pornography, only reflected their confusion. And yet the dailies merrily published reviews suggesting that these women wanted the state to shut the industry down. They didn't. They just wanted to show the ugly pictures. The ugly pictures elicited an ugly reaction that in the experience of the filmmakers was as much of an eye-opener as shooting the film itself. The Ontario Censor Board, of course, was no more generous, refusing to let the film be shown more than once for public viewing (see more on this in "Combatting the Practice of Pornography" in this section).

Writings against pornography have been met with equal hostility. Andrea Dworkin's book *Pornography: Men Possessing Women* was released last summer. The prose is tough and unsparing, laced with words like *cunt, prick* and *fuck,* because Dworkin believes that the point cannot be made by pretending that the pornographer's lexicon does not exist. In presenting her argument that pornography enforces male power, she does not take the easy route that traverses only the pornography that overtly exploits violence, but rather, she deals with all of it, making the connections between the dynamics of force and sexual objectification.

The media establishment hasn't taken too kindly to Dworkin's views. She says the only way any of the media outlets will agree to let her have her say is on a panel that would pit her against a bona fide pornographer. She has consistently refused to participate in such a circus.

I wasn't so smart. I made an attempt to espouse a feminist perspective on the pornography issue on a local public affairs program that featured Al Goldstein, the publisher of *Screw* magazine. The encounter began with a variation on the 'if you're a feminist you don't like men' theme, but this time it was, 'if you're against pornography then you don't like sex.' 'Maybe you don't like sex because you're a lesbian.' 'How dare you infringe on someone's rights when you are the advocate of perversion.'

III

We have to face the fact that the desire to disrupt the pornography industry is an unpopular stance: that resistance to the point of view is emotional and can evoke a lot of anger; that the tactics used to diffuse our arguments will be very, very dirty; and that any measure will be used to coerce us back into the cocoon of silence.

But what do we say? What do we do? We are uncomfortable with censorship and with the fact that any desire to dismantle the pornography industry is shared with interests, the moral majority in particular, with whom we prefer to believe we have nothing in common. Our hands are tied by liberals who balk at the notion of denying anyone freedom of anything and by artists who believe that their creative vision will be cramped by constraints imposed on them by an external body. For the most part, one can find a sympathetic ear to the notion that pornography is not good for women. But it is difficult to argue forcibly for solutions to the problem that don't raise the hackles of even the most progressive and well-meaning listener.

To start, I think we should stay away from the word censorship and replace it with a more acceptable term like regulation. Regulation is actually a more accurate term for what should be done with the pornography industry and speaks more eloquently to the fact that only an infinitesimal amount of pornography that the industry churns out could possibly fall under the rubric of art, which we are least likely to want to restrain.

The rest is not art, it is product, and there is nary a product on the market that is not regulated in some way or which does not have standards to which the product must conform. So, when we say that the product must not celebrate violence against women and suggest that, since we're stuck with a film censor board, it should administer that guideline, we are seeking to regulate in the same way we say that white bread can contain only so much preservative or that a lot of hot dogs can contain only so much cereal.

This is admittedly a piece of fancy verbal footwork but it helps to place the pornography industry in its proper context.

It is an industry. Why does it deserve a hands-off policy, one which is accorded to no other capitalist venture?

One main drawback to stern regulation is the degree to which the guidelines may prevent the artist from exposing the potential for erotic art. But for our purposes, this sample guideline provides no threat to a person who wants to depict graphically any sexual acts. Depiction of sexual violence would be acceptable, as long as the perpetrator of the violence is not portrayed as a hero.

I think it is curious that the defender of individual rights has enough confidence in humankind to grant each of us the right to say anything about anything, confident that the balance will come out right and promote social justice, but refuses to believe that an individual knows the difference between the glorification of violence and depiction of violence pure and simple.

Progressives worry that regulation can be used against political dissidents and anyone else who supports alternative points of view. As a contributor to *Broadside*, certainly not a mainstream newspaper, I am keenly aware of such dangers. But I can't see how *Broadside* would be threatened by a clear guideline proscribing the celebration of violence against women in film or anything else.

The other assumption of the fearful progressive is that if we let the censor at violence then the banning of everything erotic will follow closely behind; give the state an inch and it will take a mile. But think about it — the state has seen fit to regulate what comes out of the Inco smoke stack without preventing us from barbecuing in our own backyards.

In fact it's probably not an exaggeration to say there does not exist a single social policy that does not to some extent curtail individual freedom. That's because the basic tenet of our social contract is compromise. We cede rights in order to live in this world together. Yet instead of asking the pornographer to cede his rights to exploit and propagandize, we grant cold-blooded entrepreneurs the right to ply their trade even if in so doing they create a social environment that says rape is okay.

It's time to challenge the assumption that freedom is our most precious value. Freedom of speech always sounds splendid, but in reality it is precious only if it is afforded to everyone. The pornographer tells his customers that women have no right to speak, only the right to get fucked, and so the pornographer works to deny us freedom of speech. And the recent experience of feminists attempting to avail themselves of a public forum in order to discuss exactly this makes this society's freedom of speech look like something of a joke. As long as there is no real equality, freedom of speech is useful only to those who already have power.

Many will argue that if power is to be vested in anybody, the last to be given more clout is the censor board. But regulation does not have to take place only at the hands of the censor. The members of the film industry might consider some form of censure of popular directors whose speciality is the glorification of violence against women. Filmmakers might do well to throw out of their associations and academies those filmmakers who abuse their craft and eschew art for exploitation.

Other existing legislation has some potential. The courts could be used more effectively if the Criminal Code, particularly section 159 which deals with obscenity, were taken seriously. Obscenity has to be defined more clearly so that any photograph or film that makes brutality directed against a female heroic is de facto obscene.

Subsection 7 of the section on obscenity makes it an offence to depict pictorially any crime. This section has the potential to allow charges to be brought against anyone who distributes material in which the assault of women is made titillating. Assault is, after all, a crime.

Anti-pornography protesters would encounter less resistance if the image were of a Jew being led to the chambers while a swastika-adorned German jacked off, or if the porno-graphic image were of a Black being lynched to the sexual delight of a white hangman. The outrage of the Jew, the fury of the Black would be understood by cultural critics. In fact, Canada's legislators have been so moved as to devise hate lit-erature laws that ban the dissemination of material that advo-cates genocide of any group, but only on the basis of religion, creed or colour, and not on the basis of their sex. Hence, women are without equal protection. With an appropriate amendment to the law, there may be a pornography remedy here.

But either of these approaches has its problems. While it could discourage pornographers from their most gross excess-es, it could also clog the courts with case after case, conceiv-ably grinding our already moribund justice system to a halt.

If the notion of regulation either by the courts or by the 'artist's' peers or by the censor cannot be made palatable to the public, then perhaps we should allow the pornography industry to run amok and then tax it to death, both at the consumer's and manufacturer's ends. The goal would be to take some of the profits out of the industry and back into the hands of those battling the industry's influence. It would be a new kind of Reconstruction program.

Add a hefty tax to the price of a girlie magazine and pos-sibly consumption would fall off. If the appetite for pornog-raphy is so voracious that the consumer is still willing to shell out his money, then a tax on the pornographer's income might defray profits so considerably and add so much to his paperwork that he might choose to leave the business.

Such a solution places pornography in the same category as alcohol and tobacco; another vice for the state to exploit but this time with a twist. I like the idea — far-fetched though it may be — of earmarking the tax monies derived from the industry for the services that exist to mitigate the effects of violence against women. At least rape crisis centres, the shelters for battered women, and counselling services would have a greater means to undo the damage.

IV

As the pornography industry continues to burgeon, especially in the areas of kiddie porn and violence, more and more concerned observers are thinking that the most positive steps can be taken in the area of sex education, so that the pall of disgust and terror that hangs over the sexual arena can be dispelled. A crucial subject for study is the pornography and other products of media that make violence look sexy. The images in these products reinforce the power and control that the consumer wants. It is the need for total control and domination that fuels the consumer's need for pornography.

His quest for domination is doomed. He may be able to render women dependent on him for money, for status, for information — but the last frontier is the one between the sheets. While he may have a female sexual dependent, one whom by law he can still rape, he can never master her the way the pornographic image tells him he can. His quest for domination is doomed not because there is such a thing as a lesbian, or because historically men have been less artful in their sexual relations with women, but rather because sexual energy was never meant to be manipulated or used or taken away from anyone by anybody. Our erotic energy is our own, to share when we please, and for our own sake.

But the pornographer continues to rage against the power we want to keep. In the face of the barrage, we are expected to settle for the dubious assumptions of pornography's apologists. We are asked to believe that men have the right to get sexual pleasure from the image of victimized women, and that this never affects real women in the real world. We are asked to believe that the smallest amount of protection in the form of regulation of the industry works against the precious value of freedom and therefore against us. We are asked to believe that if we protest against the pornographer's propaganda we are either crazy or sexually dysfunctional. We are asked to remain silent. It is all too much to ask.

RADICAL AND RIGHT WING —
THERE'S A DIFFERENCE

Almost immediately after feminists began to protest pornography, political forces threatened by the position — from free-speech advocates to pornographers themselves — were quick to say that feminists and right wingers were in bed with each other [sic] on the issue. This was and remains an illusion.

IN 1982 The Wimmen's Fire Brigade claimed credit for blowing up three Red Hot Video outlets in British Columbia. The members of the Brigade would be extremely uncomfortable among the devotees of the church, family and decency who have taken a strong stand against pornography. Right-wingers, in turn, would be appalled to discover that their opposition to pornography was shared by anarchists, or worse, lesbian feminists, a group they would be more likely to identify as perverts in cahoots with pornographers than as allies. In the meantime, critics of the feminist anti-pornography viewpoint remain mired in the regrettable fiction that feminists opposing pornography are really Bible thumpers in extravagant political drag.

There is a good reason why confusion reigns here. Feminists and right-wing groups have been jostling over the

Originally published in *Pornography and the Sex Crisis* (Toronto: Amanita Enterprises, 1989. Reprint, Second Story Press, 1992).

same politically charged terrain — family, reproduction and sexuality — for almost a decade The conservative contingent believes that the family is the backbone of the social order. Representatives of Canadians for Decency, a group of conservatives organizing against pornography, have stated explicitly that they are family people. The family, according to the credo of the conservative, provides a tidy structure in which sexuality, male sexuality especially, can be controlled. Without the family intact, argues the moralist, male sexuality would run rampant, posing a persistent threat to the civilized status quo.

Feminists, however, see that the conservative model for the family, in which women take care of children and the housework while men take care of the real world, is hopelessly undemocratic. Men's work in the real world is paid work and carries with it a great deal more status than housework. When women are locked into unpaid work in the family and depend on husbands for money, they lose their mobility and their autonomy. The right-wing model for the family based in old traditions is an institution of inequality.

Far from being a safe place for women, the family winds up being a haven for violent men. New research shows that one out of eight women will be assaulted by the man she lives with. And another Canadian study reports that one of four women will have her first sexual experience under conditions of force, at the hands of a member of her family or someone close to it. The family has been men's private sphere for controlling women without worrying about the long arm of the law. Police are still reluctant to interfere in 'domestic disputes' lest they invade someone's privacy. Until 1983, the law gave legal protection to rapists, provided that the assailant was the husband and the victim the wife. In the end, what these protective measures do is keep not sex but sexual abuse in the family.

The right wing believes abortion is the ultimate sin and compulsory pregnancy a suitable punishment for a woman who has been sexually active. The conservative opposition to abortion is closely linked with its moralist stance on sexuality, in general that sex should be confined to the marriage contract and private behaviour and kept away from public view and public discourse. Recreational sex is lust and lust keeps people in chains binding all to the prison of their bodies, whose appetites have to be kept in constant check. Within this frame, moralists identify men as the weaker sex and more likely to yield to temptation, but it is women who are blamed for tempting them, much the way the pornographer makes women responsible for all sexual excess.

While conservatives have wanted to keep sex private, feminists are making sexuality a political issue. If the forces of decency argue that sex is intrinsically negative and has to be repressed and thwarted, anti-pornography feminists like myself say that society's mass culture with pornography as one of its most influential instruments constructs sexuality in a particular way, making it so that women are used or made powerless in the construct of dominance and submission, coercion and violence. If the forces of decency argue that sexuality imprisons us, I would counter that sexuality is not intrinsically or naturally negative. It has no nature. Instead, it has to be reconstructed with an entirely new set of values. If we do not allow the pornographer to do all the exploring for us, sexual exploration on our terms, if we can find them, will be a liberating force.

When right-wingers speak, they do so with a wistful nostalgia for a past they believe was much more simple and straightforward. But the past holds no special magic. The Western world for generations gone by has not been a particularly hospitable place for women, who could enter the work force only in demeaning low-paid jobs and who were given no role in political life, let alone a sexuality over which they might have had some control.

It's a future where women have self-determination that

feminists hunger for, and that future would, yes, include female orgasm.

Similarly, the right-wing and anti-pornography feminist views on pornography are not consonant at all. We agree only that pornography has to be fought. Underlying that, there are profound differences on the question of why.

In the mind of the conservative, pornography leads to the destruction of the family by providing an outlet for recreational sex and the expression of anti-social sexual values. But anti-pornography feminists know that the family is quite resilient and that plenty of family men love pornography. As long as the family remains undemocratic, the pornography that promotes the power imbalance between the sexes, and the family that makes a man's home his castle, are two very compatible things, part of the same social order. The way the conservative sees it, pornography excites lust, which leads to pregnancy outside of marriage, which leads to the heinous sin of abortion.

But according to the anti-pornography feminist view, pornography enshrines male control over women. This is the same control over women that is exercised when the state refuses to give women access to abortion and reproductive freedom. Pornography, according to the decency contingent, is a moral outrage depicting recreational sex; God would not want it that way. For anti-pornography feminists, pornography expresses a political fact: the power of men over women. The Lord is not an actor in the scenario except to the extent that he provides a pretext for orthodox churches to repress sexuality while giving women the unenviable choice of being either virgin or whore. That is why these orthodox churches have never really been able to foil the will of the pornographer: because both the church and the pornographer will their control of women.

It used to be that the public discourse pitted a member of the church, usually male, battling it out with *Playboy* over the right for men to masturbate. That triumvirate of repressed male villain, liberated male hero and average Joe consumer has changed and not only because feminists have started to talk about how they feel. Whereas the forces of repression used to be represented by male church leaders, women have become some of the most articulate proponents of the conservative stance. Indeed one of the reasons feminist opposition gets confused with moralist opposition is because in increasing numbers, the moralist opposition has been articulated by women.

High-profile political groups like the American Eagle Forum or the Canadian REAL Women have taken positions against pornography. Most of the time these women use the tried and true conservative arguments against public sexuality and threats to the family structure. Most of the time right-wing women think like right-wingers. But some of the time, right-wing women think like women.

For example, Nancy Pollack, the president of Canadians for Decency, will say outright that the Bible speaks out against fornication, but she also believes that pornography says something in particular about sex. "Pornography is someone to have, someone to get, someone to do in," she once said. "It's never a mutuality. In the stuff I've seen, the woman is frightened and hates it, then she loves it and that's supposed to be the way it is." Pollack may be a Christian opposed to public sex, but she also knows the rape myth when she sees it.

British Columbian anti-pornography activist Jancis Andrews is another case in point. She undertook a campaign to get the province's attorney general to file obscenity charges against Red Hot Video. During her campaign, she wrote to the provincial ombudsman that "violent pornography is misogyny using video tape as its medium and therefore should be regarded as a form of hate propaganda." In another letter to the attorney general, she wrote that "our work with the porn issue is just part of our fight for the human rights of all people, and when it is over ... we shall see the face of Christ and hear him say, 'Well done thou good and faithful servant'." Here's a woman who has a clear understanding of how pornography is used as a weapon to control women, and who awaits the moment of ultimate approval from the heavenly father! Nevertheless, though occasionally Pollack's and Andrews' visions blur around the woman-identified and fundamentalist edges, neither is a feminist. They have accepted the traditional discourse and have located themselves on the side of morality. I still say the alliance between feminists and right-wingers is an illusion.

At the same time as right-wing women have begun to ally with the forces of repression in what was once an entirely male dialogue, so too have women taken the opposing view in the traditional debate, articulating the civil libertarian position. Some of these women proudly identify themselves as feminists and believe they have devised expressly feminist reasons not to oppose pornography. But in the same way as right-wing women sometimes sound more like women than right-wingers when they oppose pornography, libertarian feminists often sound more like civil libertarians than feminists when they defend it. While attempting to give their argument a feminist edge, fundamentally liberal values continue to permeate their discussions.

These values have always been imbedded in the civil libertarian defence of pornography, a defence that rests with the claim that pornography is speech and that speech, especially when it is sexual and thus constitutes dissent, has to be protected and 'free' in a democratic society. Anti-pornography feminism challenges all of the elements in this formulation. For when the pornographer is so adept at defining who and what women can be; when he is so convincing as he promulgates the rape myth; when the pictures and words of pornography are there to arouse, and thus make male dominance and female submission seem second nature; when it sexually subordinates women in its production with the expectation that the subordination will continue in the consumption, then pornography is not speech at all. It does something. It is a practice.

Pornographers have been celebrated as freedom fighters because they trade in sex. This exalted status of sexual dissident is closely related to the conviction that society is sexually repressed, and that pornographers, with their open expression of sexuality, are liberators. In other words, it doesn't matter what the pornographer says about sex, it's the fact that he brings sex out into the open that matters. Given the array of cultural products that exploit sexuality and given the popularity of the products of pornography, one has to question the assumption that we live in a sexually repressive culture. Sex manuals and how-to books are voraciously consumed by people anxious to get the sex they believe will confer on them some kind of personal identity. There still is, of course, resistance to gay and lesbian sexuality, but the kind of sex pornographers promote — heterosexual scenarios of dominance, submission and force — are very popular, as we see from the ease with which these sexual values are mainstreamed.

Some sex liberals insist that pornography is positive precisely because society is so repressed. Unfetter sexuality, and the pornography will become less ugly, they say. According to this perspective, pornography is a marginalized phenomenon that depends on sexual taboo for its commercial success. But the pornographers no longer depend on taboo to sell their products. Indeed, far from pandering to the repressed conditions that allegedly keep them in business, pornographers have already broken down the barriers of sexual repression and are actually the active and effective agents in the creation of a hypersexualized society.

Ultimately, it does not matter what the pornographer says about sex, for he is decidedly not neutral on sexual values.

Rather than resisting the dominant ideologies of our society pornographers reinforce and construct them by turning the hierarchy of gender into something sexually arousing. Pornography is an institution, itself institutionalizing sexual inequality and other hierarchies, like racism, by eroticizing them. Seen this way, pornography does not push the boundaries of sexuality, it keeps them locked within the frame of hierarchy, conflict and violence. Far from being the purveyors of dissent, pornographers are eloquent advocates of the status quo — men on top, women on the bottom, socially and sexually speaking.

Civil libertarians who accept that pornography hurts women still insist that in a free and democratic society, even obnoxious speech has to be tolerated. Deny one person's freedom, and you establish a precedent for denying someone else's. This position is forged out of the fear that if one voice goes, permission is given to deny the voice of dissent. But this point of view assumes that everyone has equal access to the machinery of speech. In our political culture, it is the pornographer who builds his empire of propaganda and forced sex while women protest in the face of liberal platitudes. And one of the most effective agents in negating women's voice has been the pornographer, who reduces women to objects so that their credibility is undermined. I am increasingly frustrated with the deep entrenchment of liberal values that assume that just by saying everyone has equal rights, those rights will automatically materialize. The romanticization of free speech and other individual freedoms will never subvert male dominance and will instead continue to buttress existing power structures. Men in power will continue to speak while disenfranchised groups stay squeezed out. Women have to ask: Why should we let the pornographer speak when he does so much to keep us silent?

As the forces of repression meet those of expression, one wonders why oppression is left out. While observers, whether male or female, choose sides in the pornography question, other anti-pornography feminists and I redefine the terms of the debate. As Catharine MacKinnon suggests in "Not a Moral Issue" in *Feminism Unmodified* (Cambridge: Harvard Univeristy Press, 1987), the right thinks pornography is a moral issue of good and evil, when it actually is a political problem of power and powerlessness. The civil libertarian defends pornography as an idea or speech; I am fighting it as a practice of sexual subordination. The moralist says pornography unbridles male sexuality; I say it directs it. The civil libertarian wants to protect freedom, including the pornographer's. I yearn for the day when women will have real freedom to defend.

Ultimately, by questioning pornography's relationship to women, the feminist arguments wind up cutting through the tension between the two traditional sides of the dichotomy. The right-winger argues that the pornographer is a threat to an ordered society, the civil libertarian defends the pornographer's right to do so, while I insist that the pornographer is the champion of a very ordered status quo. And while the decency contingent fears the pornographer as sexual liberator, and the civil libertarian defends the pornographer as a speaker and dissident, I know the pornographer is a pimp.

COMBATTING THE PRACTICE OF PORNOGRAPHY

Soon after "Confronting Pornography" appeared, the emotion behind my first writings on pornography began to meet head on with the demands for a more coherent — even less naive — approach. Three things specifically moved my thinking. First, I began to see the importance of looking at the real lives of women in pornography and their lives in relation to consumers. Similarly, with voices of feminist artists worrying about the real effects of censorship on their lives, it became necessary to take a more hard-nosed approach to the problem of censorship and to participate in an analysis of how the process of censorship was operating in Canada. And naturally, it became almost impossible to talk about pornography without defining it. In Pornography and the Sex Crisis, *I made the argument that pornography is a practice of sexual subordination — pornographers present sexual subordination for sexual pleasure, sometimes their own, always for their consumers. A distillation of the thinking that led me to this conclusion and some early thoughts on what we might do about it is presented in this article.*

From *Broadside*, August/September 1984.

SINCE FEMINISTS MADE pornography an issue in the mid-seventies, we have found ourselves caged by an intense debate over censorship and the granting of arbitrary powers of the state. The following article gives a critical analysis of the problem of pornography and tries to begin the process of unlocking those cages, giving feminists new legal options to consider at the same time.

The Problem

The problem, put simply, is that pornography — whether soft-core, hard-core, explicitly violent, or just sort-of-violent, everything from *Playboy* to *Snuff* — can cause harm. While many women will tell you this purely on the basis of their own experience and feelings, the fact that pornography causes harm has received a great deal of support from academics — usually male, but that's the way it is in science — who have devised clinical studies to prove the point.

You may have heard about this body of work because most of the heavies in the field, like Ed Donnerstein and Neil Malamuth, were at the February Symposium on Media Violence and Pornography that was held in Toronto. And you can read about these studies in various academic journals and publications, especially the book *Pornography and Sexual Aggression* (New York: Academic, 1984). Do so, but remember that in many important ways — and despite whatever useful work has been undertaken — using guys in white lab coats as a source for information about women's lives may not be the most effective research method.[1]

Once out of the ivory tower and into the real world, we discover the actual harm pornography causes. It is easy to get the evidence. Talk to women. Surveying some of the survivors of wife assault, I have encountered women who openly confess that their sex lives changed considerably once their husbands got into pornography. The pornography, often from magazines, gave their spouses all kinds of ideas about what was sexy, and made their spouses wonder why their wives were not being sexy in the way pornographic models were sexy.

Many of these women report being forced to replicate sexual acts in the pornography. I'm not referring here to the other thousands of women who are offended at the sight of pornography and who believe in their guts that pornography puts them down. I am talking about the women who know that pornography is related to their own practices of sexuality as they are forced into them. In other words, pornography makes something happen in the bedroom.

Then there is the truth about what goes into the making of pornography. Many women, even anti-porn critics, think that pornography comes out of thin air and is transformed by some magic into 'images.' But there are real women in the pornography. In fact, you can't have hard-core pornography without the traffic in real women. If you ever have the chance to see porn, watch it carefully. Ask yourselves some questions. Who are those women in pornography? How did they get there? How come she's there and you're not? Who has to do what? Why are some women 'only' naked, while others are penetrated? Why does one woman perform fellatio on several men while others 'only' stand around and fondle themselves? Who is sleeping with the director? Who's controlled by a pimp? How many of these women are really victims of female sexual slavery?[2]

A good working text for understanding the problem is Linda Lovelace Marchiano's autobiography *Ordeal* (New York: Citadel, 1980). In it she describes how she was pimped, pushed around and forced to make *Deep Throat* (the single most commercially successful porn film, about a woman with a clitoris in her throat) under life-threatening conditions.

What is most interesting about Marchiano's story is how hard it is to get people to believe it. Marchiano says that the only thing people remember about her in the film was her smile. How could she have been forced if she was smiling? Because she was brutalized by her pimp, but he's off camera. People only believe what they see on camera. In the end, Marchiano's escape and survival tend to be used against her. If she was forced, how did she get away? (*Ordeal* tells how.) Feminist lawyer Catharine MacKinnon once remarked that the only way Linda Marchiano would be believed is if she were dead.

We've come to the crucial point. Fundamental to the understanding of the harm pornography causes is the radical, rare, provocative, laboratory-transforming, even world-changing act of believing women and what they say. When a woman says, "I didn't want him to take the picture," even if the photograph shows her 'enjoying it'; if she says, "He put the magazine in front of me and said 'do it' and when I didn't he beat me"; when she says that he'd never thought of ropes or paraphernalia, and without porn he never would have had the network to secure the toys he'd need to get the sex the porn advertises — we should believe her.

Whose Freedom of Speech Matters?

Using this as a working basis for understanding the harm pornography causes, anti-porn feminists enter the debate on censorship much better prepared to discuss the issue with women's interest as a priority.

Many people, including some feminists, worry. They say that freedom of speech is a fundamental value in a liberal democracy and to threaten that right is to violate one of the primary tenets of the social contract. But whose social contract is it? The persistence of pornography proves that the value of freedom of speech is celebrated in a world where everyone does not have equal access to that freedom. It takes training, resources, contacts, money, in particular, to 'speak' in this society and these prerequisites aren't doled out in equal numbers to men and women.

In a body politic committed to the free forum of ideas, it's the pornographer who builds his empire of propaganda and forced sex, while the three words used most effectively to silence women's outcry against pornography have been the words *freedom of speech*. And one of the most effective agents in freezing women's speech has been the pornographer, who reduces women to objects who can have nothing to say in the first place.

If we analyze how pornography is used, and how it works, pornography doesn't look very much like 'speech' at all. It looks more like a concrete practice: of defining how women can be; of convincing men that women like rape; of conditioning the consumer to fuse sex with aggression, conditioning them through sexual arousal so that they learn it in their bodies. Pornography uses women. Pornography does something.

Pornography comes out of and affects women's experience. *Deep Throat* was Linda Marchiano being abused. I think it's a good thing that feminists are taking a stand on which is more important — the pornographer's speech or a woman's life.[3]

But should the state be the vehicle for protecting women (and anyone else so victimized by porn) against the harm pornography causes? Feminist theory has been ambivalent about the role of the state, and the practice of state censorship has not done a great deal to resolve the question. In theory anyway, if pornography causes harm, then reducing pornography's saleability should reduce the amount made and so some of the violence done to women. (Note that I don't think ending pornography would end the entire cycle of violence against women that is systematic.) So you could say state sanctions of some kind could mitigate the impact of porn.

The guardians of individual freedoms (not as mindful of

women collectively) argue that the granting of state powers to restrict expression is dangerous. The state is not neutral, they say, and the powers we grant the state will be used against us, the radicals, dissidents, critics of the status quo — change-makers in general.

Let's see how it's been working so far.

Obscenity and the Status Quo

I'll begin with obscenity, the state's main attempt to cope with pornography. According to section 159 of Canada's Criminal Code, the distribution of materials that unduly exploit sex, or sex and violence, or sex and horror, or sex and cruelty, or sex and crime, violate obscenity law. Most of the court's decisions have been hopelessly skewed to create a body of law which is devoted to sex only and which tends to ignore the issue of violence entirely. It is true that the undue exploitation of sex and violence is, according to the law, obscene, but judges have tended to set up peculiar standards as to what constitutes the real combination. Often, only the presence of an erect penis will convince a judge that sex is involved at all. Although the Stephen Bornis decision in Ontario in the Rankine case (*Regina vs. Rankine, 1983*) was able to see sex without penetration and may have set some important precedents; for the most part the depiction of women gagged, manacled and with clips on their nipples, are not necessarily considered for prosecution. Nudity does not lend 'sex' to the image in the legal sense. Penetration does.

Unfortunately, this has been the extent of the feminist critique of obscenity and the litany of distressing legal precedents. In developing this critique, feminists have tried to isolate the violent material only as that which should be called 'obscene,' trying all the way to convince observers that we don't mind the sexual depictions, that we are pro-sex and that the 'sex' in pornography causes us no problems. Count this writer among those who tried to go this route and who criticized obscenity legislation which makes it illegal to depict a woman sucking a penis but perfectly legitimate to depict her sucking a gun.

But what do we do with the real facts, the ones that tell us that it isn't only the violent materials that are being used to keep women down or used as sex manuals forced on the victims of battery? What about the fact that the so-called 'non-violent' materials are often made under near violent conditions? In fact, much of the pornography implicated in the battery of women has been these so-called non-violent materials. More to the point, the items through which women are forced into sexual acts are very often soft-core items that, even given the long arm of the law, obscenity legislation cannot and will not touch.

Playboy and the rest of the girlie mags, after all, do not violate Canadian contemporary community standards, the very standards used to determine whether materials are obscene. Indeed, anyone with eyes and ears in this media-laden culture might conclude that *Playboy* is our community standard. In a sexist society, community standards are bound to be sexist and hence obscenity legislation is not likely to have a great deal of practical value.

Besides, if a judge were to decide his case on the basis of these standards, how could he know what they are in a practical sense. He may want to look at what magazines sell but that wouldn't help him determine a uniform Canadian standard. He may want to look at film classification and refer to the provincial censor boards which also establish policy according to community standards.

He won't get much help there. Consider what happened to the movie *Pretty Baby*. It was controversial because it contained sexual scenes with then twelve-year-old Brooke Shields. The Ontario Censor Board asked the film's distributor to cut certain sexual encounters; the Quebec board made no fuss and gave it a restricted rating. Saskatchewan banned it outright.

But even without the inconsistencies of the censor boards as evidence, anyone who's ever travelled across this country has to suspect that the idea of a contemporary Canadian community standard has to be something of a national joke.

The judges carry on though, and usually they decide what the community won't tolerate. This has made certain depictions become de facto 'wrong,' and has done a lot to deny minority rights, especially those of gay men whose sexually explicit materials have been the subject of a disproportionate number of obscenity cases, and more to the point, obscenity convictions. Interestingly enough, police didn't slap an obscenity charge on *Penthouse* until it ran a 1969 lesbian photo spread featuring cunnilingus — obviously simulated.

Besides, what would happen if a judge decided that a meathook in a woman's vagina does not violate community standards? Would that make the woman any less real? The business of 'community standards' makes it seem that the pornographer's crime is having the bad manners to have chosen the wrong audience[4] and that if only he could find an audience that would tolerate his battery of women, then he will have been a good citizen of our society.

In the end, our obscenity legislation does a lot more to protect the sexual status quo — *Playboy*, homophobia and the pimp's power — than it does to protect women from exploitation.

Film Censorship's Trade Off

As the debate goes on, the Ontario Censor Board's track record is growing more dreadful by the day.

Item: Lizzie Borden's film *Born in Flames*, whose screening was sponsored by *Broadside* and *FUSE* magazine, is submitted to the theatres branch and can't get a public screening unless a five second shot of an erect penis being fitted with a prophylactic is eliminated. The context is, 'A woman's work is never done,' but the Censor Board doesn't worry about context. It worries about erect penises. In the same film, an army of women on bicycles blows whistles to subvert a rape attempt. The scene, an empowering one for women, falls under the board's arbitrary category of 'threat of rape' and is given as the reason for classifying the film as restricted.

Item: the censor board has always had the advantage of having it both ways. On the one hand, the board eliminates explicit violence because the Criminal Code does not find explicit violence uncoupled with sex to be obscene. But the board also eliminates explicit sex (and erect penises) precisely because the legal precedent has found them obscene. Which is it? Filmmakers want to know. They have not been satisfied with having the board state policy on the basis of community standards which are too difficult to pin down. It was exactly this vagueness of the community standard test that prompted an Ontario court decision (in the case involving the Ontario Film and Video Appreciation Society and the Ontario Board of Censors) that the censor board policies were unconstitutional. The courts urged the theatres branch to construct clear guidelines so that film distributors would know their parameters.

This provided a splendid opportunity for the board to give some clarity. It was a time for some creative decision-making; clear-cut guidelines; a chance to change censorship policy and adapt it to real social needs. The Ontario government came back with new legislation and the Film Review Board. It was a breathtaking display of arrogance: the law changed very little and parroted the former policies, laying them down as legislative guidelines as if that would be an improvement over their in-house use only. The 'threat of rape,' regardless of context, continues to influence film classifications; erect penises and penetration, our current definition of obscenity, are still being eliminated. Rather than cashing in on feminist political support by, for example, softening the arbitrary power given to the board, and considering context, the board merrily carries right on with policies that threaten feminist artistic and political initiatives.

Item: what the government's new amendments did do was grant the theatres branch new powers over hard-core pornographic videotapes leased for home use. During the week of the announcement of the new Film Review Board, the police wasted no time before they let community artists know who's boss. They raided A Space, a video art gallery on the night A Space was screening videos on the subject of gay sexuality. These videos were neither pornographic, hard-core, nor leased for home use.

It is becoming harder and harder to shrug off these excesses as the price we have to pay to keep pornographers in line. This is not to say that the state can never be a foil for the imbalance of power that exists in a liberal democracy where the more money you have the more speech you can buy. Rather, it is to recognize that the Ontario government, anyway, is not neutral, and its practice is such that we have to conclude that the trade off — we'll let you make a few mistakes by taking away a few artistic frames of film as long as you take away many frames of pornographic film — is not working in our favour. And it becomes easier to come to terms with the failure of censorship when there is another alternative.

Human Rights Option

All of this legal lingo must not cloud our eyes for a single second to the fact that pornography is still linked to serious injuries and harms done to women. All we've concluded so far from the excess of the censor board and the ineffectual implementation or the misuse of obscenity law is that we empower the state at our peril.

But we are still left with the legal option of empowering

women instead. This is the intent of the Minneapolis Ordinance,[5] which gives women the right to sue in their own person those who traffic in the pornography that causes them harm. This is a civil rights approach to pornography that in a Canadian context could be adapted quite handily into a human rights framework.

There are three steps to this legal strategy:

1. Pornography must be defined legally in such a way as to embrace all sexually explicit depictions of the subordination of women, including those that appear in mainstream magazines. This is especially important in a soft-core pornographic culture like Canada's.

2. We must define how pornography is a practice of sex discrimination. The Minneapolis Ordinance gives us the basic language to work with (though plainly a Canadian definition would be consonant with Canadian human rights vocabulary): ... pornography is central in creating and maintaining the civil inequality of the sexes. Pornography is a systematic practice of exploitation and subordination based on sex which differentially harms women. The bigotry and contempt it promotes, with the acts of aggression it fosters, harm women's opportunities for equality in rights of employments, property rights (etc) ... promote injury and degradation such as rape, battery (etc) ... contribute significantly to restricting women from full exercise of citizen ship and participation in public life ... undermine women's equal exercise of rights ....

3. The commission of certain acts connected to the discriminatory practice of pornography allows the women harmed to sue the perpetrators of those acts,

specifically the traffickers[6] and manufacturers in pornography. These are acts, not images, depictions or things said, and they are as follows:

A. Coercion and fraudulent induction into pornographic performance in the manufacture of pornography. Anyone who forces a woman to pose or perform sexually either for a camera or an audience can have an action taken against him.

B. Assault of physical attack due to pornography. This allows victims or their agents to file suit, in addition to assault charges against the assailant and against the pornographers because the pornographers have been complicit in the crime.

C. Intrusive display. Anyone or any institution that displays pornography in such a way as to interfere with a person's right not to see it may have an action taken against him or her.

Here's how it might work. Human rights legislation that made the above practices sex discriminatory would allow women to appear before human rights commissions and file for damages against the traffickers in pornography. Whereas the rules of evidence are strictly adhered to in a court of law, they are somewhat more relaxed in a human rights setting, thus making it possible for a woman to make her case.

This doesn't mean this strategy can swing into gear without some crucial public education. We aren't as litigation-happy as our American neighbours; we have to sort out how to develop a feminist legal think-tank that can represent women and inform them of their legal rights, and not at the financial expense of the women's community. Plainly, this is a new idea that needs a great deal of fine-tuning.

But look how many problems it does solve, even in its rawest form. For one thing, the human rights approach reduces the dichotomy between public and private that is nurtured by obscenity and censorship law. Obscenity and censorship are fashioned to deal with the public face of pornography, the business going on in the public realm, and not the private acting out of pornography going on in the bedroom. The civil libertarian likes to insist on this and spends a great deal of his energy fighting for the individual's right to privacy. This public/private line is not unlike the civil libertarian's freedom of speech approach in that it tends not take into account women's experience. Women know that the greater part of violence against women takes place in private, away from the jurisdiction's official censorship, and wonder whose privacy the civil libertarian is trying to defend. If we take the route of human rights as we've outlined them here, women could redress the damages done to them even if they occurred away from public view.

Allowing women to sue for damages also does a lot to take the profit out of pornography, something many people agree would reduce considerably the amount of pornography in our world. Of course, the way to eliminate the profit is to eliminate the market, which can occur through long range solutions like sex education and wholesale changes in our sexual assumptions and practice. In the meantime, awarding damages to women is an attack on the profit incentive of pornography and actually makes the practice of pornography financially risky. It makes the distributors think twice, since they can never be sure that the pornography they are moving across the country will not be used against women in a situation of force.

And it is a great improvement over taking fines and putting them into government bank accounts, as if obscenity harmed the government. Obscenity, after all doesn't cause any harm in the first place. Pornography does. And once we've extracted the monies for damages done by pornography, we can finally put these funds where they should go — to the women who have suffered.

Now the censorship debate has been redesigned. Except for the role of a court-like apparatus like the Human Rights Commission, the agents of the state — police officers, crown attorneys, and government appointees — have been largely eliminated from the scene. They are replaced by those better situated to know the damages done: those who experience pornography in their lives. This kind of legislation does away with the potential misinterpretation by law enforcement officers and empowers women instead, all in the context of a law that favours equality.

Now is the time for these kinds of legislative changes. We are at the precise point in our constitutional history when we can take advantage of what we know about pornography. We are just now developing a social contract for Canada (in the form of our current debates on the constitution). Unlike our neighbours in the US, we do not have a 200-year history of constitutional law that has been imbedded in stone, or 'freedoms' that have protected pornographers and have posed obstacles for women fighting against pornography. We have the chance to entrench human rights in a vocabulary that is distinctly Canadian and at a time when our decisions will define the basic constitutional priorities for the future.

Think about it. This human rights approach to pornography would pose no threat to the development of alternative erotic materials; nor would such a law make sex education materials subject to prosecution; it would not allow the law to say that sex was dirty. It would allow the law to make a strong statement in favour of equality; it would make it harder for the consumers of pornography to think their sex-discriminatory practice had anything to do with freedom; it would allow women who are dehumanized in the making and consumption of pornography to reclaim humanity through court action.

And it would, you can bet on it, cause a great deal of trouble for pornographers.

Who Would Have a Case?

1. The family of Barbra Schlifer. Her rapist/killer explained in court that he had a pornographic magazine in his hand as he cut her open.

2. Vanessa Williams. Nineteen eighty-four's Miss America was forced to give up her title when nude photographs of her appeared in *Penthouse* against her will. She claims that the release form was never signed (even *Playboy* representatives, explaining why they refused the photos, have stated that all was not well with the release form) and that the stated intentions of photographer Tom Chapel were to photograph Williams in silhouette only. This is a classic case of coercion and fraudulent induction into pornographic performance.

3. Any female medical student who finds herself looking at a pornographic slide in the middle of an anatomy class (a favourite joke among anatomy professors) could file suit against the professor and the medical school for intrusive display.

4. Any person forced to look at pornography while in the process of paying their bills at a variety store would have a case against the proprietor for intrusive display.

5. The hundreds of women who are forced to replicate sexual acts in pornographic materials will finally be empowered to sue the traffickers of the pornography for violation of these women's human rights.

A definition of pornography as developed by Andrea Dworkin and Catharine MacKinnon in the Minneapolis Ordinance:

Pornography is the sexually explicit subordination of women graphically depicted which also includes one or more of the following:

1. Women are presented dehumanized as objects, things or commodities; or

2. Women are presented as sexual objects who enjoy pain or humiliation; or

3. Women are presented as sexual objects who experience pleasure in being raped; or

4. Women are presented as sexual objects tied up or cut up or mutilated or bruised or physically hurt; or

5. Women are presented in postures of sexual submission; or

6. Women's bodies are exhibited such that women are reduced to these parts; or

7. Women are presented as whores by nature; or

8. Women are presented being penetrated by objects or animals; or

9. Women are presented in scenarios of degradation, injury, abasement, torture, shown as filthy or inferior, bleeding or bruised, or hurt in a context which makes these conditions sexual. (The use of men, children or transsexuals in the place of women above is also pornography.)

UPDATE 1995

As women's voices began to redefine the pornography debate, they had a surprisingly strong impact on Canada's legal machinery. Forcing pornography onto women — especially in the workplace — began to be viewed as a form of sexual harassment. Several cases involving pornography have come before the Ontario Human Rights Commission. And as early as 1983, in the *Rankine* case especially, decisions began to show more concern with violence and less concern for sexual materials and a startling receptiveness to the idea that harm and pornography may be linked. I consider this, by the way, a sign of feminism's growing influence and I celebrate it.

It was, in part, this increasing elasticity of obscenity law that led the Legal Education and Action Fund (LEAF — an organization committed to legal strategies that advance women's equality and, in particular, those that relate to the Charter of Rights) to intervene in the case of *Regina vs. Butler* and to make the argument that materials that were dehumanizing and degrading should be called obscene. In a groundbreaking decision, the Supreme Court of Canada accepted the terms, stating specifically that such images may be considered undue exploitation of sex and that it was reasonable to assume that there is a causal link between exposure to such images and changes in beliefs and attitudes.

By the time the decision came down in February 1992, feminists were still so torn by the issue that few noticed even a small triumph. Many anti-censorship activists complained that LEAF was setting the wrong priorities and supporting censorship. I agree that obscenity law in Canada has been used as a pretty blunt instrument, but political opinion in Canada shows no signs of wanting to dismantle Canada's censorship machinery. And the courts have consistently rejected civil libertarian ideas when they have been used to argue that obscenity laws violate Canada's Charter of Rights. This has been true from the *Butler* decision which reaffirms that obscenity constitutes a reasonable limit to freedom of speech, right up to the latest round, in which defence lawyers for artist Eli Langer (See "Kids as the Object of Art" in this section) were unable to convince the judge that Canada's child pornography violated individual or privacy rights. So for the time being our censorship machinery is here to stay — let the system reflect our concerns.

What I like about the *Butler* decision is that it takes the accent off sexual explicitness (penetration, for example). That's a huge step forward from a law that to all intents and purposes made it nearly impossible to develop sexual materials that analyze and resist the rape culture's dominant sexual ideology and practice.

Yet, feminist sceptics have remained. It hasn't helped that in its implementation, the newly designed obscenity law continues to be used to harass gay and lesbian materials. Most notably, the first post-*Butler* obscenity charges came down against *Bad Attitude*, a magazine of so-called erotica made by lesbians for lesbians. It is painful to witness the continued persecution of gay and lesbian materials, especially in the face of the myriad materials that exploit women made by men for men.

But I have to ask the question: If gay and lesbian materials do subordinate women, should they be exempt from legal scrutiny? When I think about sexual materials made by lesbians for lesbians, I ask the same questions I ask about the vast majority of straight pornography — Who are these women? How did they get there? How come they're there and I'm not? In the case of the *Bad Attitude* materials, it was S/M scenes and piercings that were targeted. I'd rather they hadn't been. I can say that much. But I can't say that I want to fight for the right of women to hurt other women in sex.

NOTES

1. For a review of this data see "Pornography," Chapter 1 in *Pornography and the Sex Crisis* (Toronto: Second Story Press, 1992).

2. As Kathleen Barry defines it in her book *Female Sexual Slavery*: "Present in all conditions where women or girls cannot change the immediate conditions of their existence; where regardless of how they got into those conditions, they can't get out; and where they are subject to sexual violence and exploitation."

3. MacKinnon discusses this in her paper "Not A Moral Issue," originally delivered to the February Symposium on Media Violence and Pornography, Toronto, 1984. Now published in *Feminism Unmodified.*

4. Ibid.

5. The Minneapolis Ordinance was an attempt to amend the Minneapolis Civil Rights Ordinance to include pornography as an act of sex discrimination. The Minneapolis Ordinance was passed by the City Council, vetoed by the mayor, then reintroduced and defeated, then reworded, introduced and finally passed, then vetoed again by the mayor. The last section of the article is based — sometimes loosely, sometimes closely — on the Minneapolis Ordinance, and is an attempt to adapt the ordinance to a Canadian context.

6. The Minneapolis Ordinance includes 'trafficking,' the implications of which are complex and, though I don't oppose including trafficking as actionable, the topic warrants another article.

BIBLIOGRAPHY

Ed Donnerstein and Neil M. Malamuth, eds. *Pornography and Sexual Aggression.* New York: Academic, 1984.

Andrea Dworkin. *Pornography: Men Possessing Women.* New York: Perogee, 1981.

Andrea Dworkin. *Right Wing Women.* New York: Coward-McCann Inc., 1983.

Catharine MacKinnon. "Not a Moral Issue," a critique of American pornography, is published in *Feminism Unmodified.* Cambridge: Harvard University Press, 1987.

SENSATIONALIZING CENSORSHIP

I used to begin conversations about what pornography is and does by insisting that we have the discussion without once using the word censorship. Let's pretend we're not going to do anything about pornography, I'd say. Let's just talk about what it is. I did this because I sensed what I call future tense panic — the tendency to deny that a problem exists because of what might be done about it. Censorship is always the biggest fear, of course. But while anti-pornography activists have often been accused of sensationalizing women's pain and overstating women's victim status, defenders of free speech have been known to exaggerate every now and again, too.

WHEN I RECEIVED a letter from a Toronto art gallery encouraging me to oppose Bill 82, the Ontario government's attempt to increase the province's censorship powers over film and video the letter was of great interest to me. I have been critical of Bill 82 since its introduction and I continue to be intrigued by the ways in which the anti-censorship movement, and even the mainstream press, are describing the way censorship is taking place in Canada. I would like, once again, to add my voice to the chorus of opponents to the province's legal initiatives. But I also want to lodge a public complaint against the manipulation of language and ideas

---

Originally appeared in *Broadside*, July 1985.

that occurs in the debate on censorship, and to draw some important distinctions.

Language is loaded. Words like *ban, censorship,* and *resistance* pack a powerful emotional punch and I think they are being abused by anti-censorship feminists and non-feminists.

Let me start with the word *ban.* During the Six Days of Resistance film festival in Toronto in April, film and video artists exhibited work they either refused to send to the censor board or refused to cut when the board demanded eliminations. The six days of 'previously banned films' were held to protest increased film censorship powers. The strategy was a good one. There were so many artists committing this act of civil disobedience that it was hard for police to disrupt the event (they did not). At the same time, the public got a chance to see exactly what the state censors don't want us to see. And we got a chance to see the work of artists who would not dream of submitting their work for scrutiny to the censor board. Still, the word *ban* is not an appropriate way to describe the history of these films and videos. For one thing, many of them were never sent to the censor board in the first place.

Recently, the *Toronto Star* used the words *previously banned* to describe Louis Malle's film *Pretty Baby.* This isn't accurate. The film was supposed to be screened at Queen's University and was not. What had happened is that the board wanted scenes cut from *Pretty Baby.* Malle refused. *Pretty Baby* eventually was approved for screenings in private, or by invitation, which was eventually the treatment given to the anti-porn film *Not a Love Story.* This may have been inconvenient, discriminatory, unfair, a violation of Canada's charter of rights, or reactionary, but an outright ban it was not.

The use of the word *resistance* when referring to the struggles against the censor board, is chosen, I suspect, to aggrandize political activism against the theatres branch. The word evokes the struggle against political oppression, and obviously the artists resisting during the six days believe there is as much at stake for them here as is at stake in countries where ban means 'show it and you'll be imprisoned and tortured' and where resistance means having to carry a gun. I think using the word *resistance* romanticizes their refusal to collaborate (another loaded word) with the censor board excesses here in Ontario which can, to be sure, be placed on a continuum of state authoritarianism. But really, a $500 fine slapped onto the resisters who resisted — expressly, I might add, so that censor board powers could then be tested in court — cannot be breathed in the same breath with the experience of those who cannot speak against state interests without winding up in jail.

Malcolm Dean, the author of *Censored*, a vituperation against censorship and one of the centrepieces of Canadian anti-censorship argument, can only criticize the Ontario Board for being sexually uptight and a little silly, and we can count on the fingers of one hand the cases of outright repression of political views that he's able to come up with — hardly a litany of oppressive censorship.

I have a problem with anti-censorship activists trying to analyze the actions of the censor board as direct political actions against political radicals. The treatment given to *Not a Love Story* and *Born in Flames* was not an attempt to repress political ideas, but the result of the board's arbitrary standards that do not take context into account; an erect penis is an erect penis, and must be eliminated, regardless of what the directors — Bonnie Klein and Lizzie Borden, respectively — had to say about the social meaning of a stiff phallus. It's not feminism that is being censored but erect penises, and surely they are not the same thing.

Of course, we need to depict sex in order to offer a critical analysis of sexual politics and thus the board's obsession with sexual images and the failure of the board to recognize context does get in the way of the presentation of feminist ideas. But that is different from saying that dissidents are the first to get slammed for censorship. This may seem like a minor distinction but it's an important one for feminists seriously trying to grapple with the way in which the state does function against our own expression. What we should be doing is unpacking the term *political oppression*, making sense of it in the context of sexual representation and figuring out how the censor board winds up silencing us with its arbitrary views on sexuality. Many anti-censorship feminists have acted on a commitment to do just that. But sometimes they do so with the 'they're out to get us' attitude that misses the point.

The paranoia often gets in the way of clear thinking. In the letter I received from the Toronto gallery, the author explained how writers should be worried, too. To wit: "The banning of Margaret Laurences's book by the Board of Education is a case in point."

This is almost silly. The Board of Education in Peterborough did not ban *The Diviners* — high school kids can purchase a copy of the book at bookstores in their communities. The board did question whether the book should be in high school libraries. This is not censorship, unless you think that if your child were taking James Keegstra's (a notorious neo-Nazi) class in Alberta, your right to say, 'Don't teach *Mein Kampf* to my kids' is censorship. What is taking place is a serious battle between the rights of parents and the rights of the state to determine what ought to be taught in the classroom. It is profoundly distressing that there are parents who want to keep the insights of Margaret Laurence's art out of the hands of their children, but their right to do so is what is in question here. It is, in fact, quite a sophisticated political conundrum that can't be reduced by using fright words like *censorship*.

UPDATE 1995

Recent developments in Canada have engendered a new wave of anti-censorship hysteria that is polarizing the pornography and censorship debates in disturbing ways. Two developments in particular have given rise to righteous anger over excessive state powers — the obscenity charges laid against the lesbian sex magazine *Bad Attitude* in the wake of the precedent-setting *Butler* decision on obscenity and subsequent hassles of gay and lesbian bookstores by customs. Also vexing fighters for freedom of speech is the confiscation of Eli Langer's paintings depicting children in scenes of being sexually abused. (See more on Langer in "Kids as the Object of Art" in this section.)

In the *Bad Attitude* case, Canada's obscenity law had been given a jolt when the Supreme Court ruled that sexual materials that were dehumanizing and degrading could be obscene. This shifted obscenity's emphasis off the undue exploitation of sex and on to a concern about pornography's actual harm. The first to be charged under the new decision was *Bad Attitude*, proving anti-censorship activists' long-standing claim that gay and lesbian material is always the first to face censorship.

Similarly, Canada Customs officers, who weed and detain materials based on whether they feel they violate obscenity standards, continued to hold back scores of books from gay and lesbian bookstores like Little Sisters in Vancouver and Glad Day in Toronto. Tired of the aggravation from customs, Little Sisters has filed a discrimination case against customs. The decision is pending.

Taken together, the events have touched off countless handwringing articles about the fate of sex and freedom in Canadian culture. Both *The Toronto Star* and *The Globe and Mail* featured lengthy features — upwards of 200 inches each — on the front pages of their influential Saturday arts sections bemoaning the heavy hand of the state. In these and in other shorter columns that cropped up to complain, you can get a sense of how the anti-censorship hysteria is building. *The Toronto Star* art critic, for example, had the nerve to report that there was no evidence to support the claim that pornography and male behaviour connect. Note that he doesn't say that studies linking violence against women with pornography have problems with the methodology or the reasoning. He sneers that 'there isn't a shred of evidence.' He doesn't even say that violence and pornography don't connect. He says that there's no link between pornography and male behaviour.

Just what is the male orgasm promoted by pornography, if not behaviour — speech?

As for the reports on the *Bad Attitude* case, almost nobody who wrote about it ever saw the materials — I did — or bothered to say that the materials featured lesbians in S/M activities. This is not to say lesbian pornography should be called obscene, only that reporting on the bust without mentioning the contents of the material is a little more than misleading. It makes it look like customs is targeting gay and lesbian sexual materials regardless of their content, deeming anything gay or lesbian dehumanizing or degrading, per se.

In the US — where the liberal establishment defends freedom of speech with religious conviction — writers have had a field day with this situation. Magazines from the *New Yorker* (October 1994) to the lesbian chic *Deneuve* (May 1995) have delivered lengthy features on the lessons to be taken from Canada's experience.

The *New Yorker* piece was plainly undertaken as a cautionary tale, but even in it, Janine Fuller, operator of the Little Sisters bookstore that came under customs fire, could only say that Customs had not yet got around to implementing the *Butler* decision and that that was the problem.

At the same time, the hyperbolic responses from anti-censorship advocates here in Canada have fed their American counterparts' I-told-you-so smugness about what happens when you give the state any authority. Especially interesting is the recent release by Nadine Strossen, president of the American Civil Liberties Union, who checks in with her confrontationally entitled book, *Defending Pornography* (New York: Scribner, 1995). It contains a hunk of material on Canada, designed to show the slickness of the slippery slope — open the door just a bit to the state and it will barge in and take over — and how feminists will inevitably be burned by censorship.

I understand that Strossen is just doing her job, which is to take freedom of speech to its absolute max — even if it means defending pornography. But her zealousness gets in the way of truth. At one point, she makes the wacky claim that the dominant target of Canadian censorship has been materials headed for gay, lesbian and feminist bookstores. She comes to this conclusion in part because that's what gay and lesbian bookstore owners told her — and she didn't see fit to check it out — but also because it suits her argument. Note that nowhere has anyone developed data to suggest that the numbers of confiscations of feminist, gay and lesbian materials has significantly increased in the post-*Butler* environment. Canada's censorship machinery has always discriminated against gay and lesbian materials. Unfortunately, the *Butler* decision did not change that.

I called Revenue Canada for a list of materials that had been detained at the border since 1992 and received a list of hundreds of publications. Perhaps 5 percent were gay, lesbian or feminist, including the likes of *Swank Lesbians,* a division of *Hustler* magazine and hardly on the cutting edge of social change.

When I published a column in *NOW* magazine (March 23-26, 1995) complaining about Strossen's book and its use of scare tactics to support her case, I was ridiculed in the letters page — something to which I've grown accustomed whenever I write on the subject. One letter wondered whether I knew that customs had engaged Vancouver bookstore Little Sisters in a court action. Didn't I know persecution when I saw it? The writer in this instance was plainly influenced by the anti-censorship craze. She claims that Revenue Canada had taken the bookstore to court, when in fact, it was the bookstore that took Revenue Canada to court, arguing that detaining gay and lesbian materials is a practice of discrimination.

Another letter derided my efforts to get information out of Revenue Canada. Wasn't it naive to look to the oppressive state as a source? I found this typical of anti-censorship paranoia and the tendency to view as clever conspirators those bureaucrats charged with implementing Canada's censorship guidelines. I've sat with Revenue Canada reps and watched them do their jobs over the fifteen years I've researched pornography. They work like dutiful drones, looking over magazines and marking up the ones that offend the guidelines. Savvy tricksters they are not. In my own recent case, it took the Revenue Canada rep five minutes to fax the lists — hardly enough time to manufacture them. Why would he? He didn't even know why I wanted them.

Aside from wreaking havoc with reality, anti-censorship hyperbole gets in the way of our understanding the complexities of these issues. As a lesbian writer, I've been silenced myself when a poster for my play, *A Fertile Imagination*, was removed from a public building in London, Ontario. The play is about a lesbian couple preparing for motherhood and the poster featured a graphic of two nude women flying in an embrace. I was angered by the decision, but in the end I realized that the experience didn't feel as painful as those described to me by women used in pornography.

Absolutists like Nadine Strossen line everybody up behind their lines, building alliances in the most noxious places. She says our right to speak depends on the rights of pornographers to exploit. Sometimes she says pornography is good for us. She suggests too that sex workers may be on the cutting edge of women's liberation. I think we can value personal expression without defending pornography. I think we can say that prostitutes deserve to work in dignity without saying that prostitution is just like any other job. I think we can worry about censorship *and* about exploitation in the sex trade.

And contrary to the doomsayers who say these points of view spell the end of erotic life, many of us maintain them and actually continue to have sex.

KIDS AS THE OBJECT OF ART

I'm always struck by how easy it is for people to see the children in pornography as victims and how difficult it is for them to see force and coercion in pornography that features women. And this is why I don't focus too much on child pornography. It's easy to upset people with it. Why don't people get as upset over pornography that features women? Because some money's been exchanged? Does that erase the pain of the experience? Is it because she's smiling? But there's a child smiling in this picture here. What is it about the circumstances of a female's presence in pornography that changes when she turns eighteen?

Still, examining child pornography can lead to a better understanding of how pornography promotes violence against women. In child pornography, children's sexual abuse is recorded, and then the document is passed on to a consumer. Survivors of sexual abuse often report that child pornography was used to introduce the idea of sex to them. Sexually abused in the home this way, many girls run away and hit the streets. You can see why tricking for money would be a step forward for someone who has had her body stolen from her. And surely a pimp her own age might be more interesting than her father, or going out and picking up a john better than having to lie in her bedroom waiting for the doorknob to turn. If she continues in the trade — and here we come full circle — she

Originally published as "An Obscene Lack of Accountability" in *Herizons*, Winter 1995.

could turn up in pornography, which, in turn, will be used against a young girl somewhere else.

Many offenders take pictures of their victims while they are abusing them or after. In fact, having this record has particular meaning to the abuser. Only in pictures can his victim stay as young as she was at the time of the assault. Pedophiles exchange pictures. They connect by the Internet.

Canada's child pornography laws make it illegal to possess materials showing children in sexual situations. As is the case with much obscenity law in the West, artistic merit is accepted as a defence. In December 1994, a startling development took place when police laid child pornography charges against artist Eli Langer and the gallery hanging his portraits of children in sexual scenes with adults. The issue touched off a firestorm of controversy over artistic freedom. To me, Langer's is obviously a case of misplaced censorship, but it also brings up questions about public space and a gallery's responsibility to the community.

THE TROUBLING LEGAL wrangle over representation, child pornography and Eli Langer's art has turned into such a snarl that my stomach has gone into empathetic knots over the situation. Here's how I see it as a longtime anti-pornography activist.

Last December, the Mercer Union gallery in Toronto mounted a show of paintings and drawings by Toronto artist Eli Langer. The paintings depicted children being sexually abused by adults. *Globe and Mail* critic Kate Taylor reviewed the show, describing the paintings in a way that twigged the police to the possibility that the works might violate child pornography laws. These laws make it illegal to possess materials that show children in sexual situations.

Within days the police descended and busted the show, charging both the gallery and the artist under the pornography law. The charges were eventually dropped, but the crown proceeded with a hearing of forfeiture, in which the paintings themselves were placed on trial. The decision is pending.

What a mess. The worst part of it all is that we're engaged in a dreary debate over censorship instead of talking about the issues of child sexual abuse the artist intended to address. Langer told me just after the first charges were laid that the work came out of experiences with people close to him who had survived child sexual abuse. He did not disclose to me as a survivor himself and his work for the most part features girls being assaulted, but I got the sense that the creative act was in some way part of Langer's own healing process.

It turns out that Langer's interest is in the complex responses of children who know they are being violated, who sense that they are being betrayed by an adult who is supposed to love and protect them. They feel powerless to change the situation they despise, even as their bodies may be responding sexually. For the record, Langer made it clear to me that he is against sexual abuse. Now why isn't this coming out loud and clear as the debate rages around the country?

The easy answer is that the police moved in so fast and heavy-handedly that the public debate never got past the censorship issues to the ones dealing with abuse. And you could argue that Taylor was more than a little naive to goad the police. But I'm interested in what could have been done to get the work shown and talked about, without getting it busted in the first place. From that perspective, I'd say that the gallery — the institution responsible for exhibiting the work publicly — didn't do a good enough job.

The exhibit was a quickie fill-in for another show that canceled suddenly on the gallery, and consequently, Langer's show did not go through the gallery's regular curatorial process. Langer himself may not have noticed. Young and inexperienced, this was his first show; he had never before taken so much of his work into the public realm.

Given all this, you'd think the gallery would have grasped the sensitivity of the material in both the legal and the emotional sense. Why not hold a forum to help launch the show? The artist doesn't necessarily have to speak; he's already done his job. But by leading a public discussion, the gallery could have acknowledged the political work that helped open the door to these memories of abuse. After all, if it hadn't been for the years of groundwork that pushed these issues into the public consciousness, Eli Langer's work would not have been conceivable.

Connecting with the community also would have defused the censorship problems, because at the very moment of the bust, anti-pornography activists like myself would have paid a personal visit to police to tell them this is not what we had in mind.

Mercer Union went the other way. The gallery put out a smarmy press release, printed in pale, miniscule type, that passed the work off as images "dealing with children's sexuality without the compensation of consent." Pretty coy, I think.

It's worth noting too, that there were no materials given out to gallery visitors to tell them that the work was about child sexual abuse. What about an art lover who walks in off the street? She could be a survivor. Shouldn't she get to know what's going on before having to confront these images on the walls of a gallery? It makes you wonder, especially when the show was scheduled just before another exhibit, this time of lesbian pornography (the artist's term) by Shona Edelman. I question a process that has enabled both gallery and anti-censorship activists to use Eli Langer without acknowledging the real intent of Langer's work.

I define pornography as the sexually explicit subordination of women and children in pictures and in words, produced for the sake of sexual gratification. I've seen some of Langer's work — including the most extreme images of a young girl with semen dripping from her mouth and it does not meet my pornographic standard. For one thing, it's not sexually explicit in the legal sense: it suggests but does not depict penetration. Real children were not used as models. Real experience was. Most important, there is absolutely no doubt in my mind that the work was not intended for sexual gratification.

There are deep problems with the child pornography law, since by merely depicting trauma, an artist runs the risk of getting busted. But, don't be fooled into thinking that the law is the only ass around here.

Update 1995

In April 1995 the court released Langer's work citing that it had artistic merit. But the judge did reiterate that Canada's child pornography laws did not necessarily violate the Charter of Rights and that the public should continue to debate these issues through the courts.

Langer was slated to exhibit these works in the fall of 1995 at Mercer Union, but pulled the show after conflicts with the gallery. The gallery wanted to highlight Langer's censorship problems by including a special media exhibit on the trial and by adding an essay solicited from a prominent Canadian anti-censorship activist to the catalogue for the show. Langer, tired of being forced once again onto someone else's agenda, would not agree. He says that his issue is child sexual abuse and not censorship.

III

PROSTITUTION

SEX WORKERS WONDER

As women began to voice concerns about pornography, sex workers began to worry. They began to worry about how the sexuality debate was unfolding and how it was going to affect their real lives. Many workers had a stake in protecting pornography. Pornography is the high end of the industry, safer and slightly more lucrative. A porn film, for example, might take a day to make, but retakes with the same partner can feel easier than selling sex to fifteen johns a day. Many sex workers did not want to be seen as victims only and started to develop new ideas, such as, that prostitution might be a considered choice for some women. More important, prostitutes have every reason to be suspicious of anyone who wanted to put their faith in the law — laws have always been used against them. If we base our ideas on women's experience, then listening to the voices of women organizing the sex trade becomes an important part of our discovery process.

In Canada, laws prohibiting soliciting got the teeth knocked out of it in 1987 when one judge ruled that soliciting had to be pressing or persistent to be actionable. In response to the rule, the government drafted Bill C-49 which made it illegal to communicate — in whatever way — for the purposes of prostitution. The effects on prostitutes were dramatic.

Prostitution is the issue that let me discover a political and personal truth — that two things can be true at the same

Originally published as "Tramping on the Sex Trade" in *NOW* magazine, December 17-23, 1987.

*time. It's hard not to notice who's buying and who's selling.
So I think prostitution is an institution of male dominance.
But I also think prostitutes have the right to do their work in
safety and dignity.*

THE HEAT IS definitely on the prostitution trade from both
police and residents, and prostitutes' rights groups are mad
about it. They contend that property values are becoming
more important than people and that residents' reactions are
a perverse response to a perverse law that can do nothing to
end the problems associated with prostitution.

Typical of the new activism of ratepayers is the strategy of
the South of Carlton Community Association in Toronto.
During the past three weeks, members have been prowling
the streets at night wearing bright white sweatshirts screened
with an image of a woman leaning into a car. Masks give
them a menacing appearance that startles passers-by. But
what looks like a belated Halloween celebration is a concert-
ed political action intended to disrupt the transactions
between prostitutes and their clients.

The association has formed to combat what it sees as the
detritus of the prostitution trade — noise, harassment, condoms on the lawns, excrement on the lawns, even sex on the
lawns. If the police aren't going to do anything about it, argue
the residents, we'll do something for ourselves.

They began the campaign by jotting down the licence
numbers of johns cruising the streets and then started taking
pictures of men approaching prostitutes. Rather than participating in the association's version of Candid Camera, johns
began to steer clear of the area. The media loved it all and
with every one of the association's forays into the streets, camera crews swooped in with the quasi-vigilante group to record
the encounters. So intent were they to get the story that one
crew filmed an association member screaming at a tree when

there were no prostitutes to be found on the street. And a zealous City-TV reporter included in her report a clip of residents harassing a woman who was not a working prostitute.

While the media dutifully tailed the residents' groups, police officers during the same period began to sweep up johns like so many dustballs on a worn carpet. Then last week, judge Lorenzo DiCecco sentenced seven men convicted of soliciting to a street cleanup job for the South of Carlton Community Association, an unprecedented move that proved that the South of Carlton residents' profile had moved from the street to the courtroom.

DiCecco has developed a reputation for his caprice on the bench. Only six months ago, he ruled the section of the Criminal Code under which the seven men were charged (section 149.1) unconstitutional. Prior to his most recent example of creative sentencing, he had sentenced a man convicted of wife assault to write "I will not beat my wife again" one thousand times.

This time, though, DiCecco went even farther beyond the traditional parameters of sentencing procedure. In most cases, a judge sentences convicted people to community work over a particular period of time and it is left to the probation officer to decide which community organization should benefit from the activity. In this case, however, DiCecco stated specifically that the convicted johns had to work for the South of Carlton Community Association and named association spokesperson Sandra Jackson as the person the cleanup crew must report to during the completion of the sentence. At least two of the convicted men elected to forego the garbage collecting and instead donated a total of $1,600 to the Association.

"It was our idea," says Sandra Jackson, speaking for the South of Carlton residents group jubilant about the Carlton coup. "These men were donating $200 to the Salvation Army on their way into sentencing hoping to influence the court action, but we said, 'Why don't they pick up after themselves?'"

While it is already unusual for a judge to decide who ought to reap the benefit of community work, the South of Carlton group winds up being a particularly weird choice for beneficiary of the court's munificence. The group is entirely ad hoc in its structure, an absence of organization some say is designed to make them difficult to sue. The group has no constitution, no bylaws, no recorded membership, no executive, no phone number — in short, no accountability.

Not surprisingly, organized prostitutes and their supporters are furious at the latest developments. The Canadian Organization for the Rights of Prostitutes (CORP) has been attempting to represent prostitutes' interests ever since the federal government began debating bill C-49, its draconian anti-prostitution law. Val Scott, a spokesperson for CORP, feels that it has been bad enough being harassed by the police. Now the ratepayers are getting in on the abusive action.

"You go through the political process, you write your briefs, you have your meetings, and then they give the cash to the lynch mobs," she says with a mixture of frustration and resignation.

This is not the first time Toronto's streets have been inundated by angry residents taking the law into their own hands. Three years ago, alderperson Chris Korwin-Kuczynski led Parkdale residents on what was called Hooker Patrol to rid Queen Street at Bellwoods of its booming prostitution trade. Customers for commercial sex were bullied and badgered by Parkdale denizens whose actions were intended to convince police to crack down on the trade.

The Parkdale action group, along with residents in other Canadian communities, pressed for the easy solution — a law that would work. In their view, the existing statutes banning soliciting were not being enforced strongly enough. Police then found themselves further handcuffed when a BC lower court judge ruled that soliciting had to be pressing and persistent in order for police to be able to lay charges.

In the wake of the Fraser committee report on pornography and prostitution and in an effort to beef up law enforcement, the federal government passed the infamous Bill C-49, which made it illegal to communicate for the purpose of prostitution. Entrenched as section 149.1 of the Criminal Code, this is the law which DiCecco's johns were convicted of breaking. Indeed, since passage of the bill, the police have gone on an arresting spree, increasing the number of soliciting charges this year by over 100 percent.

"The whole idea of Bill C-49 was to plug the loopholes led by Judge Hutt's decision that soliciting had to be pressing and persistent to be charged," says Darlene Lawson, executive director of the Elizabeth Fry Society, an agency that offers support services to women in conflict with the law.

Lawson is angered by the Cabbagetown residents' tactics. "So now three years later, we have Bill C-49 ," she says. "And we have screaming residents who are just as angry and just as vocal. We have more convictions at great cost to the taxpayer, and prostitution hasn't gone underground or gone away. In fact, criminalization exacerbates these problems and creates new ones."

One of those new problems, ironically, is the presence of prostitutes on Cabbagetown's Seaton and Ontario streets.

"There wouldn't be any women working on the side streets of Cabbagetown if it weren't for Bill C-49," says Scott. "We can't work the well-lit track on Isabella because the yellow cars tell you to move out. Once the people from the suburbs have left the downtown core we can go back, but that's not until two a.m. If the residents were truly concerned about prostitutes leaving the area, they should be lobbying for a government solution that will work for everyone, and that is decriminalization."

In the meantime, residents meet with police officers who meet with politicians, while no one meets with the prostitutes themselves. Lawson wonders why the South of Carlton residents have gone their particular route.

"Perhaps instead of throwing eggs and verbal abuse, they could have talked to the women about the condoms on the front lawns, the traffic congestion and the other problems. We sit down with other parties, parties involved in much more destructive criminal activity to work these things out. Environmental polluters sit down with environmentalists and unions, therapists sit down with child sexual abusers to figure out what we can do for them, and yet in the middle of this raging controversy, prostitutes are given no voice."

This, Scott insists, will not change until people start thinking of prostitutes as human beings.

"The media has made the residents' activities more of a circus than a political action," says Scott, "and then when they put these lynch mobs on TV, they turn them into heroes, reinforcing the idea that it is all right to abuse and harass prostitutes. We know what's really going on when these activities are referred to as a street cleanup. It means that everybody thinks we are garbage."

The way things are going, adds Lawson, the real agenda of the residents' groups is being obscured. "In this case, it's not a moral issue," she says, "it is not an issue of violence against women, it is not a religious issue or a health issue, it is an issue of property values." In fact, it is not a coincidence that Sandra Jackson, the spokesperson for the South of Carlton Community Association, is a real estate agent for Darrell Kent Real Estate, the realtor that led the gentrification of the Cabbagetown district. The Cabbagetown uproar is reminiscent of the shutdown of the Yonge Street massage parlours, an initiative for which Cadillac Fairview and Eaton's lobbied fiercely as a prelude to the construction of the Eaton Centre.

Jackson insists that it is the quality of life her group wants to improve but she admits that, "It makes it difficult to sell houses on the west side of Parliament, more difficult than other houses in Cabbagetown that don't have street prostitution. Many clients have said to me they won't buy there."

Lawson doubts the motives of the residents. "In my views" she says, "the attitudes of the residents play into the hands of politicians and police officers. They are short-sighted and narrow. You have to be unaware of the systematic reasons for prostitution to think that criminalization and increased police activity are going to resolve the problems associated with prostitution."

Scott adds that as long as soliciting is criminalized, prostitutes do not have equal protection under the law. Getting them off one street only drives them to another less well-lit area where women are even more vulnerable to rape and assault.

A report just completed for the Elizabeth Fry Society comments that Bill C-49 is making it impossible for street prostitutes to talk to each other about bad tricks and their own safety. Police keep breaking up the groups of women who are discussing imminent dangers, imagining that the women are talking about money and where the action is. And Scott insists that keeping soliciting criminalized is a good way for police to maintain ready access to informants.

"That way they can pump us for information about what is going on in the streets. Working girls see a lot that police would like us to tell them about."

Staff inspector Jim Clark of the morality squad insists that implementation of the law and some heavy fines will provide the means to eliminate prostitution.

"Bill C-49 is a good piece of legislation," he says. "If you can create the deterrent, the numbers of people buying will shrink. We did a sweep last Friday and the numbers are already down."

But not for long, say those who work closely with street prostitutes. Charging prostitutes and fining them only perpetuates a pattern that guarantees that the women will end up back on the pavement. "Those women are out there because they have to be," insists Christine Semia-Weinstein, program director for Street Outreach Services, the Cabbagetown agency that tries to meet the needs of women on the street. "Then you charge them, and they get criminal records which make it harder for them to find other jobs. They have no marketable skills. If you fine them $150 and then expect them to raise money for lawyers' fees, the only way they can do that is by going back out on the streets to raise the money."

Lately, police have begun to alter their street strategy, letting prostitutes off the hook and concentrating on sweeping their customers. In 1986, police laid 1,187 charges. This year they have laid 649 charges, almost half of which have been laid against johns. Late last month, after a three-day sweep, police laid 442 charges, all of them against men. "The program used to be split between females and men," says Clark. "But the reason why there are so many women out there is because the demand is so high. We think that like any company, if we can do away with the market, the company will go away."

But CORP members question the motives behind the new strategy. Johns, they say, have been chosen as the legal target because they tend to be more docile, legally speaking. They plead guilty to speed up the court actions, and are far too frightened of the risks of public exposure to take the radical route of challenging the constitutional validity of the law.

The prostitution trade is characterized by its own class hierarchy in which escort services make sex available at a high price while street prostitutes charge much less. The police sweeps are not at all threatening to the prostitutes working the upscale trade. So life may get a little easier for crown attorneys, but it is getting much tougher for the women on the street.

"It'll be boom for the escort services and hell for the girls in the streets," contends Scott. "Who knows where the guys who can't afford escort service prices will go? A lot of people think that by charging the tricks, it equals everything out. We see it as equal oppression, and we don't see that the oppression equalled out is any better."

A number of factors could possibly turn the situation around and lead to a slowdown in police activity. Simple economics, if they are ever considered, dictate that the crackdown won't last forever. Although police will not reveal the exact extent to which their resources are being depleted by their nocturnal vigils, it is doubtful that the scores of squad cars and staff devoted to the project can remain on the prostitution case for too much longer. Prostitutes know that and are waiting out the police crackdown until the heat eases and they can hit the streets again.

Taxpayers, too, may get fidgety when they begin to do the accounting for the prostitution patrols. *The Hastings Law Journal* reported that American cities are spending astronomical amounts of money on prostitution 'cleanups.' The tab runs anywhere from $2 million in Philadelphia to $10 million in Dallas and, according to the report, prostitution has not vanished in any of these city centres.

Already, some of the residential tide is turning, and not all Toronto ratepayers are cheering the police on. Last week, Ward 4 alderperson Tony O'Donohue held a meeting of residents at a public school in his riding to whip up sentiments similar to those of the South of Carlton Community Association. He discovered that his constituents were not all in favour of sicking the police on the prostitutes. At least six times during the proceedings, community residents stated the need for social services and opposed moving prostitutes to another community. According to Lawson, those vocal residents are on the right track. "Services like Parkdale Legal Services, Street Outreach Services, Hassle Free Clinic and the Elizabeth Fry Society are trying to create the relationships of trust with prostitutes that will ultimately work to increase their concrete options," she says. "We know that choice counts and that treating people like human beings instead of trash will get us somewhere. And if we remove the legal stigma against prostitution, at least these women won't continue to be considered the scum of the female gender."

WHISPERING OUT LOUD

WITH THE POSSIBLE exception of the one on pornography, the prostitution debate within the feminist movement has been one of the most bitter any of us had ever experienced. It's not surprising that prostitution and pornography should run neck and neck in the pain sweepstakes: both issues compel us to consider the meaning of sexuality in our culture. And when sexuality is the issue, people get mad. Three years ago, at a feminist law conference in New York (Women and The Law, 1986) prostitutes' rights groups ganged up on anti-pornography feminists in a shouting match I thought I would never witness within the feminist movement. And then at the so-called feminist conference on prostitution called Challenging Our Images sponsored by OPIRG (Ontario Public Interest Research Group) in Toronto, feminists like myself who were trying to say that prostitution was an institution of male dominance were confronted by sex workers who had decided that anti-pornography feminists were to blame for everything: bad laws, social stigmatization, the madonna/whore syndrome — just about every factor in prostitutes' real oppression.

Tired of being classed as victims only, organized sex workers don't want to be singled out in the continuum of women's experience. They now openly question whether there's much real difference between the prostitute/client relationship and

From *Broadside*, February 1989.

the relationship between husband and wife — except that prostitutes are more open about the exchange rate. They suggest that, given the range of choices, and the amount of money to be made, prostitution might be a fair choice. Feminists, they say, are just uptight because the commodity marketed is sex.

As the discourse has continued, I've become acutely aware of what is subverting radical feminism's credibility on the prostitution issue: our voices do not ring true. Most of us simply cannot speak with the authenticity of the first person. This means that when sex workers say that they experience tricking as 'just another gig,' or 'no worse than being a secretary,' or 'a job I want to do but in safety,' there isn't a lot we can say. For what do we know? We have never been there. We may know what it feels like to be sexually violated. We may feel that having a penis somewhere inside of us does not feel the same way as having to type a manuscript or work the check-out counter. We may know that it's not sex that's for sale but a woman's lived-in body. But if a fundamental principle of radical feminists is to believe women and what they say, we have no way to respond to sex workers who just want to be left to do their work in peace and safety.

So it's left to ex-prostitutes — ones who use the word *escape* to describe their leaving the sex trade, to do so in their own voice and to fight for their space in the debate. That's sometimes been hard. At the 1986 conference in Toronto sponsored by OPIRG, prostitutes' rights groups threatened to pull out if the conference became anything other than a forum for them to challenge what they thought was feminist thinking on the subject.

But one ex-prostitute did come and she produced a magic moment at the conference. After a sex worker described how hooking helped her live out her sexual fantasies, the woman stood up and said, "Oh, come on. I've been there. Don't tell me that every time you give some guy a blow job you get off on it."

"Well, not every time," the sex worker agreed. "You're right. Sometimes it isn't fun being flat on your back in the back of a car."

It was one of the few moments during the conference when reality triumphed over rhetoric. I learned something from the exchange. It became obvious to me that only ex-prostitutes could bridge the gap between sex-critical feminists and prostitutes' rights groups. And how I wished that Sarah Wynter had been there. Wynter is a member of Women Hurt in Systems of Prostitution Engaged in Revolt (WHISPER), a collective of ex-prostitutes organizing to respond to the myths about prostitution that have permeated our culture and feminism and to challenge the authority of prostitutes' rights groups who, according to Wynter, are not telling the truth about what it's like to have to sell sex.

"We started to organize because the cultural mythology didn't reflect the reality of our lives," she said during a recent visit to Toronto. I'm referring to the line that prostitution is a free choice; that it can be decontextualized from the patriarchal society we live in; that it can be fixed by unionizing it, legalizing, decriminalizing it; that the relation between a pimp and a prostitute is a love relationship; that prostitutes are on the cutting edge of women's sexual liberation and that prostitutes control tricks and the rate of pay. Johns don't pay you so you get sexual pleasure. They pay you to use your body. I think it's a mistake to validate it.

"I was sold into prostitution and control of my life was taken away from me. I learned that prostitution is an abusive institution that benefits men. The pimp gets money, the john gets sexual gratification. Prostitution gives men access to women and children sexuality limited only by men's ability to pay. I've yet to meet a prostitute who hasn't experienced some kind of abuse. That's why we founded WHISPER, because we knew that women whisper about the things that happen to them."

Wynter's experience makes it hard for us to take at face value the claims of prostitutes' rights groups who say that selling sex is like selling any other skill. And while prostitution critics have been called theorists who dwell in the abstract, Wynter says it's the prostitutes' rights groups that aren't taking reality into account.

"Your boss doesn't beat you up if you don't type up a manuscript. A waitress doesn't get raped by the restaurant patrons. Saying that giving blow jobs to men is a great job is a bunch of crap." As for sex workers, collectives: "When your job is to get fucked, that's what you get, and you can't make it better by getting a union.

"I'm bored and disgusted with prostitutes' rights groups that want to reclaim the word *whore*. I don't want to do that any more than I want to reclaim the words *bitch* or *cunt* or any other name men give to our oppression. How would we react to a completely house-broken slave who insisted on us calling her nigger? We wouldn't be able to get the word out of our mouths."

Where she does agree with prostitutes' advocates is in their opposition to misogynist laws. "No woman deserves to be abused. The legal system is abusive and constructed to uphold male interests."

But unlike the NAC (National Action Committee) prostitution committee and social service agencies working with street women, she does not support the repeal of laws that make it illegal to live off the avails of prostitution. Prostitutes' rights groups say that such laws make it impossible for sex workers to live with their lovers. Wynter doesn't buy it. "Look at the books and tell me how many pimps are rotting in jail. This is a smoke-screen to protect pimps."

When pressed about the dilemma of wanting to believe women when they describe their lives, while not being able to fathom the liberating qualities of selling sex, Wynter takes a strong stand. She makes the parallel between prostitutes who say they like their work and their pimps, and assaulted women who insist that everything in their marriages is just fine.

"There are battered women who say, 'Johnny didn't mean to hit me. He hit me because he loves me. I deserve it.' We said no one deserves it and if you would like to think about this and do something different, come to the shelter and we'll support your choice.

"Prostitution is paradigmatic of women's subordinate status in the culture. Until we deconstruct that, nothing's going to change. I was working in feminism long before I founded WHISPER. If you believe that feminism is about creating social change for women and about deconstructing patriarchy, then we can't have much to do with anyone who supports patriarchy because they don't have time to topple it."

UPDATE 1995

WHISPER maintains its mailing address at:

Whisper Lake Street Station
Box 8719, Minneapolis
Minnesota, USA
55408

WOMB FOR RENT

Though prostitution has usually been defined as the selling of sex, new developments in technology have created a new form of sex trade, the selling of women's bodies for reproductive purposes. The case of Mary Beth Whitehead, the recalcitrant surrogate mother for the Sterns, broke ground both legally and in terms of public consciousness. Feminists began to sense that surrogacy contracts were fertile ground for female exploitation and rallied to Whitehead's support. We can get a sense of where public opinion lay on the matter, if only by how the case has been named. It's referred to as the Baby M case. Melissa was the name the Sterns gave to the newborn. Mary Beth Whitehead called her Sara. So why haven't we called it the Baby S case?

WHEN KARL MARX coined the term alienated labour he wasn't thinking about what has become known as surrogate motherhood. But as infertile couples pine for children and poor women look for new ways of making money, the phrase is taking on new meaning. More and more reproductive contracts are being signed in the US and birth mothers are preparing to carry babies for nine months, only to hand them over forever to waiting couples.

This piece blends "Pondering the Problems of Paid Female Fertility" from *NOW* magazine May 21-27, 1987, and "Womb For Rent," from *Broadside*, May 1987.

This is viewed in some quarters as the ultimate virtuous maternal sacrifice, but not everyone is happy with the new developments. The pope wasted no lime in denouncing surrogacy and other forms of reproductive technologies in his last encyclical. The Vatican reaction thus inverted the church's anti-abortion clarion call of 'no sex without babies,' making it 'no babies without sex.'

In March, a New Jersey judge made history when he granted custody of the child known as Baby M to the Sterns, the couple who had contracted for her birth, and not to Mary Beth Whitehead, the baby's natural mother. The story of Mary Beth Whitehead and the court's failure to grant her custody of her daughter Sara prove two things that feminists had already suspected: make it possible for a woman to lease her uterus, and women with dreams of increased financial security will do so; place the interests of the sperm donor beside the interests of the birthing mother donor, especially in a court of law, and male interests will prevail. Janice Raymond, a radical feminist, refers to surrogacy arrangements as a "reproductive ménage à trois" in which two women do the bidding of one man; Andrea Dworkin, in 1982, anticipated the new trend to surrogacy with a grim vision of women in cages, some enslaved for sex, some enslaved for reproduction. Feminist sociologist Margrit Eichler has already petitioned the federal government for a royal commission on surrogacy. And Phyllis Chesler has been active and vocal in her support of the now notorious Mary Beth Whitehead.

It was Mary Beth Whitehead's custody battle with William and Elizabeth Stern that thrust the issue of surrogate motherhood into the public consciousness. In the middle of her pregnancy, she changed her mind and when the baby was born refused to give up the child. When police took the child away from her, she filed a suit for custody, which she lost when New Jersey superior court judge Harvey Sorkow granted custody to the Sterns. But even taking the warnings of feminist philosophers into account, we can be astonished at how vividly Whitehead's story evokes the gender interests behind surrogacy.

Whitehead, at the age of twenty-eight, decided that she wanted to bear a child for someone else in exchange for financial compensation. She wanted to do something nice for someone. She had two children of her own, both of whom she had conceived as a teenager. She thought bearing a child would be a good thing to do as a more mature person, to do it right. The money appealed to her as well. She and her husband Richard thought that the money could be used as an investment in the college education of their children, or for a down payment on another house. Richard Whitehead, a sanitary worker, supported his wife's decision to enter into a reproductive contract. He had had a vasectomy.

Whitehead then found Noel Keane. This was not difficult, since Keane had already built up a high profile through his so-called infertility clinic.

Like most prospective womb-leases, Whitehead was interviewed by a psychologist who was supposed to determine whether Whitehead was suitable. The psychologist expressed doubt on the assessment form that Whitehead would be willing to surrender the child after birth. For the record, it should be made clear that there has almost never been a woman who has entered into a surrogacy contract who has said she found it easy to give up the child after birth. But the psychologist determined that Whitehead would have more than average problems with the surrender. In spite of the extravagant claims of infertility clinics that biological mothers are screened assiduously before signing a contract, William and Elizabeth Stern were never informed of the contents of Mary Beth Whitehead's psychological file.

That, by the way, was the end of Whitehead's counselling encounters. Although other clinics build in a counselling component with the birth mother, Whitehead received no counselling of any kind, least of all from anyone with the experience or the sensitivity to guide her through the emotional intensity of the pregnancy.

The Sterns may not have seen Whitehead's file but they did meet her and actually chose her, possibly because the resemblance between Whitehead and Elizabeth Stern is so uncanny. In any case, they interviewed her before entering into the contractual agreement.

The agreement itself is truly astonishing. Modelled after marriage agreements,the reproductive contract had no adversarial qualities built into the process: Whitehead never had her own lawyer. The contract was negotiated by lawyers for Noel Keane.

Keane himself still stands firm on the claim that women come to him with total comprehension of what is going to happen to them. Consistent with right-wing women's appropriation of feminist ideas — as in 'giving respect to homemakers is an issue of equality' — Keane puts a clever spin on the politics of reproductive freedom.

"Feminists are divided about the issue," he says. "They fought for years for women to the right to control their reproduction and to do what they want with their bodies. I'm just helping them do that."

But, in fact, with no one there to represent her interests, Whitehead signed everything away — what she could eat, drink, any control over her body. Even control over her emotions was negotiated — the contract stipulated that Mary Beth would not love the baby she was carrying. By the time Whitehead's signature was on the dotted line, she had significantly less legal protection than birth mothers who are considering relinquishing their children under New Jersey adoption law. The financial arrangements are even more chilling. The Sterns were obliged to pay Whitehead $10,000, which translates, not counting sleeping hours, to $1.56 per hour. Unlike most one-term contracts, which arrange for half the funds up front and the other half upon completion of the agreement, birth mothers get their fee only on delivery.

The silent partner in the deal is, of course, the surrogacy broker, in this case lawyer Noel Keane who is one of the largest operators in the US.

Payment was to be delivered to Whitehead but only if Whitehead delivered a baby acceptable to the Sterns. If she miscarried she was to be remunerated $1,000. If amniocentesis revealed problems with the fetus, Whitehead was obliged to have an abortion and to be remunerated $1,000. If she delivered a stillborn child, she would receive $1,000, though Keane says in many contracts that figure can go up to $3,000. If she delivered a child with defects, she would receive $1,000. It is not clear whether the Sterns could have rejected the child, and paid only $1,000 if they didn't like the colour of the baby's hair. The Sterns' $10,000 was kept in escrow by the Keane clinic. The Sterns were paid the interest during the pregnancy.

Obviously many women are so financially strapped that they are willing to take the risk.

Keane is less interested in the ethics of the matter. He's there to represent the contracting couple. When asked how he could countenance, in the case of a woman bearing a still-born child, paying her $7,000 less for doing essentially the same work, he offers the law's bottom line: "Because she agreed to it."

Lucky for him. He charges $7,500 for every arrangement he makes. In addition, a $5,000 insurance fee was paid by the Sterns in case of a medical emergency, bringing the total cost of the contract, including payment to the mother, to the director and to the insurance company, close to $23,000. Whitehead would have received $1,000 if something went wrong. Keane was to get his fee no matter what.

Keane completed his 160th reproductive transaction a year ago, and boasts that he now arranges seven or eight per month. Keane's clinic earned $600,000 last year.

Phyllis Chesler, author of *Mothers on Trial*, was among those who spearheaded the daily demonstrations that took place outside the New Jersey courtroom in support of Mary Beth Whitehead. Chesler calls Keane's fee profit. Referring to Keane as a pimp, she charges that under present conditions, reproductive contracts give economically privileged couples access to economically disadvantaged women. She says she can't help noticing who's buying and who's selling and questions the idea that women enter into these agreements as equals.

Toronto lawyer Phillip Epstein agrees. He has helped couples complete surrogacy agreements. But he confesses to some unease. "It's a business I discourage," he says. "Many couples come to me seeking advice about how to proceed with these kind of things. By the time I get through the problems — the costs, risks, the whole process, the intrusions of the press, what to tell the child about the conditions of birth, the possibility that the birth mother will show up later — the couple usually changes their mind and decides not to go through with it."

That leaves Epstein with completing legal documents for arrangements begun without him and which involve couples coming to him with the pregnant mother to sort out the legal details. Most of the couples are Canadians who have contracted with American women, and there are open immigration and citizenship matters to resolve.

"There are only two reasons why a woman would want to enter into this kind of arrangement: the money or the desire to be pregnant. I'm taken aback at how much $10,000 means to people. They believe it can get them out of any financial difficulty, and no, I've never known a wealthy woman to want to become a surrogate mother for money."

Chesler describes the class contours of surrogacy this way: "The majority of women who enter these agreements with couples are younger, uneducated, poor — certainly in comparison to those buying — the economically disenfranchised who believe that this is all they can do. It is like prostitution, because women sell their bodies. But it is different from prostitution in that by agreeing to this type of arrangement, they can be a good girl instead of a bad girl."

But as Chesler suggests, there are ways that surrogacy looks alot like the experience of prostitution. "These women are saying, 'Hurt me and it won't touch me.' They seem to be behaving like abuse victims who are used to powerful people coming into their lives and taking away what's most important to them. If this is a model for female mental health, look out for us."

Seen Chesler's way, Mary Beth Whitehead is a rebel and heroine.

According to the agreement, amniocentesis was mandatory: a clause which even the hostile judge Sorkow saw fit to deem unconstitutional. The contract still does, however, demand that a woman not smoke, drink or take prescription drugs without the clinic doctor's approval. It also insists that mothers be available for interviews with doctors on demand, and still stipulates that the birth mother may not develop any emotional attachment to the fetus. In her fourth month of pregnancy, when Whitehead was obliged to go for the procedure she began to have doubts about the whole arrangement. She did not want to have amniocentesis. She did not think it was necessary, since she was only twenty-eight years old, and she worried about what would happen to the baby if she went ahead with the procedure. Keane's representatives made it clear to her that she had no choice: she had signed a contract. Whitehead believed them. She had no lawyer of her own to tell her otherwise. She went through with the amniocentesis, but she was already getting so angry that she withheld information from the Sterns about the sex of the baby. This has been called vindictive behaviour by some news writers.

Less than one week before Whitehead gave birth, Keane

phoned her to tell her that one of the legal instruments required for surrogacy had not yet been executed. Whitehead had signed the contract with the clinic, but she had not yet signed the agreement terminating custody rights of the child. Whitehead gave birth to Sara in hospital with her husband at her side. The Sterns were not present. By then, Whitehead had already decided she would not give up the child. She signed the birth certificate naming the baby Sara Elizabeth and identifying Richard, her husband, as the father. It was Noel Keane who told Whitehead that since the paperwork was not complete she should take the baby home with her. At that point, Whitehead had not signed any relinquishment papers, and had received only a small stipend for maternity clothes and similar expenses. She never, during these events and those that followed, received any payment for conceiving and birthing the baby.

A few days later, Whitehead allowed the Sterns to take the baby home with them but she immediately regretted the decision and took Sara back the next day. She phoned Keane to tell him that she could not go through with the terms of the contract. He seemed unfazed by the news, and assured Whitehead that the worst that could happen was that the Sterns would demand visitation rights.

But the Sterns proved more demanding. They went with the police to the Whitehead's house to take the baby back. The police demanded that Whitehead give them Melissa Stern. Whitehead said that there was no such person there, that the baby she was holding was Sara Whitehead and that she had the papers to prove it. She then made an excuse to leave the room with the baby and handed the child out the back window of her bedroom where Richard, with whom she had hatched the plan, was waiting for her. She then returned to the Sterns and the police to tell them that she didn't have any baby any more. The police took Whitehead and threw her into their cruiser where they handcuffed her. The Sterns stood by and watched. The police finally realized that without the paperwork, they did not have any legal grounds for taking the baby away.

After the violent episode with the police and with a new awareness that the Sterns were growing more ruthless, the Whiteheads moved to Florida to be with Whitehead's mother. Hearing news of the move, the Sterns put a lien on the Whitehead's house in New Jersey, making it impossible for the Whiteheads to move back in or to rent or sell their property. It was at that point that the much publicized phone call took place between William Stern and Mary Beth Whitehead.

The transcripts were filed as evidence against Whitehead during the custody trial. Distraught after the police harassment and furious at the Sterns for jeopardizing access to her property, Whitehead asked, "Why are you doing this to me?" Stern who had made the call expressly to tape it, urged her to calm down. "What do you want me to do, kill myself?" she asked, while Stern's tape rolled and he muttered, "Now, now." "Do you want me to kill the baby?" she asked, at which point Stern no doubt sensed a real triumph.

Many of Whitehead's supporters have given sympathetic interpretations of the conversation, but generous readings are really not required. Whitehead was angry and hurt, and spoke as if she were. Why wouldn't she? She didn't know Stern was taping her.

While Mary Beth Whitehead was in the hospital with a viral infection, five police officers came to Whitehead's mother's home, knocked her grandmother to the ground, took the screaming baby from her crib and fended off her older sister who, with a hairbrush, was striking at the officers' knees, screaming, "Don't take my baby sister." The Sterns were at the police station and as soon as they received the child, filed for custody of the baby.

Throughout the controversy the press never took much

to Whitehead. Perhaps they just plain didn't like her. Maybe they identified more with the professional couple William and Elizabeth Stern who ultimately got custody of the baby they had contracted for. Either way, after the announcement of Sorkow's landmark decision, the Sterns appeared at a press conference where the members of the press gave the Sterns a standing ovation.

The press' infatuation with the Sterns may explain why so much information has been distorted by news reporters. Once journalists were through with the story, the public was given the distinct impression that the very respectable and sane Sterns had been traumatized by an unstable and dangerous woman. Looking back on the facts of the situation, the set up — from the surrogacy clinic through to the police involvement — looks much more like a case of hands on control over Whitehead and actual violence against her.

The Sterns were portrayed as forebearing heroes with legitimate desires for a child. Much has been made of the fact that William chose surrogacy over adoption because he wanted to continue his family lineage. He had no living relatives because his family had been slaughtered in the Holocaust. This has gained him some support from some Jews whose sympathies for the survivor would likely subside somewhat if they understood that William married a non-Jew, sought a non-Jew as the biological mother of his child, and intended to raise his daughter Unitarian; William Stern's Judaism is in his genes.

And, contrary to public perception, his wife Elizabeth is not infertile. She diagnosed herself as having a palsy that might make pregnancy dangerous. She did not want to take the risks.

Toronto psychologist Paula Caplan, author of *The Myth of Women's Masochism,* agrees that the press were hopelessly biased. But she also thinks it is impossible to talk about reproductive contracts without recognizing the rampant misogyny that defines public attitudes and which left Mary

Beth Whitehead with virtually no mainstream support.

"Some people say, 'She's carried a child before this [Whitehead already had two children.] She should have known,'" complains Caplan. "But people don't say that to people who marry a second time. They don't say, 'You've done this before so you have to stay together.' People tend to be selective about who they make these demands of. It's ironic that most of the time in the course of my work, I am fighting people who say biological motherhood is beautiful and wonderful and that women should do only this. Where are these sociobiologists, those great intellectuals and psychiatrists now? They are not supporting Mary Beth Whitehead."

But whatever went wrong with Whitehead, according to Keane, does not happen very often.

"In 160 cases, I've only had three that didn't work out," he says. "My attention has been brought to no other cases. There are times when a woman changes her mind, like in a marriage. I guess if the screening process could be improved, then that's what we would be aiming for. But as it is, we are just starting to perfect the systems and, given the amount of time we've been doing this [Keane got into the business in 1972], the situation isn't all that bad."

"Well, I've met with some of them [Keane's surrogate mothers]," says lawyer Epstein, who has completed surrogacy contracts for Canadian couples transacting with American women, "and they are not all that happy. I talked with one who tried to commit suicide after the birth and who has been in counselling for the past two years. Keane doesn't know about these things because he doesn't do all that much follow-up. All he sees is the woman handing over the baby and walking into the sunset."

While lawyers sort out the legal ramifications of the case, feminists scramble to support women who may be exploited and entrepreneurs defend their business practices. But the quiet sorrow of infertile couples remains. Epstein's experience, though, has led him to the conclusion that the dilemma of infertility may not be a shared one. Echoing Raymond's metaphor of the reproductive ménage à trois, Epstein says the vast majority of cases involve the man providing sperm to the surrogate, rather than the couple providing a fertilized ovum for implantation.

"In most of the situations I've encountered," says Epstein, "the husbands have been much more keen than the wives. It's the husbands who are pushing the genetic connection, and they usually have a macho attitude about it."

"This ought to be the time for people to ask some questions about adoption in general," says Phyllis Chesler. "Questions about genetic narcissism, about how difficult it is for people to take responsibility for children who aren't related to them genetically, about the racism involved when people refuse to care for non-white babies and the callousness exhibited when people reject children that are 'slightly used.'

"There is no question that the sterility of women is an increasing problem. We should be looking at what makes women sterile: the toxicity of the environment, the damage done to women by birth control devices, especially the Dalkon Shield. We should be looking at what's causing the problem, not plundering women's resource of fertility to solve it."

UPDATE 1995

Noel Keane continues to be America's premier surrogate broker, operating what he calls a worldwide surrogacy service out of Indianapolis. His surrogacy headquarters were moved there when courts in Michigan and New York made the practice of surrogacy illegal, though Keane continues to operate a law practice, without surrogacy contracts, in his home of Lansing, Michigan.

In Indianapolis, the price of the service has gone up. It now costs a total of $45,000 for a couple to set up a surrogacy arrangement with Keane taking $16,000 per contract. He reports having participated in 600 births with 200 pending. Estimating his yearly output at 150 cases, he boasts that business at the clinic brings in well over $1-million per year.

Phillip Epstein continues to practice law in Toronto, though his misgivings about surrogacy have served to limit his involvement.

Mary Beth Whitehead has remarried and has two children with her new husband.

IV

MEDIA,
CULTURE
& SEX

Unmasking the Media

I became interested in media literacy after spending many years researching and writing about sexual violence and its connection to pornography. The pornography work can be extremely demoralizing. The more I talk about it publicly, the more likely it is that a woman will disclose an abusive experience to me after the lecture. The more sexual abuse is studied, the more we uncover. The more we look at media images, the more reinforcement we see for the sexual violence that is so distressingly pervasive.

Consider these depressing statistics: one in ten women living with her spouse is beaten by him; a woman is raped in this country every seventeen seconds; one in four women will have her first sexual experience with a member of her family or someone close to it before she is sixteen and under conditions of force. A new study on pornography indicates the majority of consumers of these advertisements for sexual subordination are teenaged men.

Helping sexual violence victims get on with their lives in the wake of the devastation has always been feminism's priority. Educating the public to care, and getting the government to fund crisis centres is essential short-term work. But what about the long term? We need strategies beyond crisis intervention that refuse to assume that sexual violence has to exist. Media literacy can be one of those strategies.

Originally published in *Forum: The Magazine for Secondary School Educators*, December 1987/January 1988.

AN AD FOR Impulse perfume features a woman taking the escalator at the Eaton Centre shopping mall in Toronto. As she goes up, a man passes her going down. He is so enthralled with ... something that he races to a flower store, buys a bouquet, and chases after the woman. He finally catches up to her and hands her the flowers. She smiles her appreciation.

In a grade twelve classroom, I asked the students what they thought about this ad. "Here's something for the girls in the class to consider," I offered. "What would you do if a man you didn't know started chasing you through the Eaton Centre?"

"I'd be terrified and I'd split, as fast as possible," said one girl, rolling her eyes.

So began an essential process of media literacy in the classroom: distinguishing between fantasy and reality, discussing why advertisers eschew real life for fantastic romantic situations. But the discussion did not stop there.

"Wait a second," said one of the boys, somewhat truculently. "Don't tell me if a good-looking guy started pursuing you in a mall, you wouldn't like it. If a good-looking girl started coming after me I would be thrilled." He grinned.

"Well, it's different for us," said another girl. "It's just not the same."

The sparks began to fly as these students discussed the meaning of media images and whose point of view the images tended to represent. For in the Impulse ad, though the woman was the main focus, the entire narrative unfolded from a male perspective. Crucially, while the students sorted out differences between reality and fantasy, they engaged in an energetic conversation about sexual violence. From their conversation, they discovered women fear it, men do not. They shared differences. With a few nudges from me, they were able to see that a nude stranger presenting himself to a woman is seen as a threat, while a nude stranger who presents herself to a man is seen as an opportunity.

This interaction is typical of the way media literacy may

be used to approach the issues of sexuality and violence. The media strategy depends on a number of assumptions. First, it assumes that media have an enormous influence on young people. Studies have provided some startling data, including the fact that $500-million of advertising in the United States is directed at children under the age of thirteen. And we know that many students, possibly the majority, spend more time in front of the television than they do in the classroom.

This brings us to the second assumption imbedded in media literacy: kids love media, especially the images marketed for them specifically. Discussions of media — how they are created and what they are made for — can provide students with insights into how the economy works, what market research is about, and how teens are often targeted as the market for these products. Media literacy begins by accepting that media are a fact of life and then uses media images as an appealing way to get students to talk about social values.

Let me give another example. In a session with high school students in grades ten to thirteen, I showed a dozen slides, all advertisements in *Vogue* or other fashion periodicals. The ads were slick, imbued with splendid production values, and very vivid. As soon as the first slide went up, I suspected we would have a successful session. Most students, including many of the boys, recognized the ads, were able to identify the item being marketed, and sometimes even took the time to say what they thought of the product. This easy recognition acted as positive reinforcement for students who prided themselves on having this kind of information, who consequently felt their interests were being validated, and who were thus more willing to get involved in the discussion.

An advertisement for jean products featured a couple lying on the beach. The man's hand lay casually on the woman's buttocks and her jean jacket was open to give the impression she had nothing on underneath. The class looked at the slide and began to 'deconstruct' the image. They suggested that the man's hand on her back was a gesture of possession, that the couple's positioning was not exactly equal — the woman's entire body was directed toward the camera and she was made to appear significantly less clad than the man. These perceptions came from the students themselves and, for the most part, were astonishingly astute.

I then asked why they thought women were often depicted half-dressed while men in the same images appeared fully clothed. Said one student: "Because women are always expected to be sexy." "For whom?" I asked. "And why?" And we were off.

During the same session, we looked at two photographs: a head-and-shoulders shot of a man and one of a woman.

"What," I asked, "did each of these people have to do to their faces to get ready for the day?" Starting from the top of their heads and working down, we made a list of activities (hairwashing, shaving, etc.), the products they would use, the amount of time they would take, and the amount of money the products would cost. Naturally, the list for the woman was significantly longer in terms of both the number of products and the time it takes to apply them. And of course the woman's cosmetics agenda was much more expensive.

This was a tricky discussion because while the object of this exercise is to uncover sex differences, it can also potentially alienate the girls for whom cosmetics are extremely important. But give young women the opportunity to discuss the differences between makeup as mask and makeup as a personal expression of creativity and it gets interesting. The boys were fascinated anyway. They'd never heard girls talk about their motivations or their interests in these kinds of things. Other slides depicted scenarios conveying the message that violence was attractive and sex was especially exciting if an element of menace or danger was present. Some magazine ads sexualized young children, making them appear older and sexually appealing.

"Why can't kids just be kids?" asked one forlorn student. "I don't like being pushed around," said another girl. In these situations, the girls were usually more forthcoming than the boys and there was no doubt the value of violence was being questioned intensely by these young women. As for the boys, even if they were not anxious to talk, they were experiencing a challenge to the pervasive message that women like a small shove every now and then.

Less than ten years ago, the term *rock video* was unknown. Now rock video has become an essential element in record marketing and there are television stations devoted solely to rock video airplay. In its first year of operation, the Canadian MuchMusic station attracted more subscribers than station managers had expected to garner in five years, surprising even the most experienced market analysts. Equally astonished were the producers of rock videos, who discovered that, during certain times of the day, the main audience for these three-minute advertisements for popular songs were children aged nine to thirteen.

Unlike ads for cosmetics and clothing, rock videos are directed primarily to a young audience that has always had a special affinity for popular music. They believe this music belongs to them and their loyalty to favourite rock groups is fierce. This affinity may be harnessed in deconstructing rock videos with fascinating results. When the subject is rock video, its content and meaning, students are ready to talk. They are also prepared to listen to descriptions of the process of making a rock video. They understand that the idea is to market pop performers, using images to complement the power of the music itself. What they may not know is how much the videos cost, who makes the artistic decisions about how the video will look (they are often surprised to hear that the musicians frequently have no input whatsoever), and how rock videos are marketed (unlike other forms of advertising, record companies do not have to pay for air time). In sessions with students about rock videos, we begin with these basics pertaining to the recording music industry.

But it is the deconstruction process that is always the most dynamic. My own method of deconstruction is inspired by feminist and feminist-influenced critiques of art, image, and their social construction. John Berger's *Ways of Seeing* is particularly useful for elucidating the point that women are surveyed by the male gaze and E. Ann Kaplan's book *Women and Film* contains a groundbreaking essay, "Is the Gaze Male?," that elaborates on this concept. A third book about art and its institutions, *Old Mistresses* by Rozsika Parker and Griselda Pollack, analyzes how art is valued and by whom. Together these books provide the groundwork for understanding both the basic elements of feminist film theory: analysis of the content of an image, its narrative and its characters, and analysis of the values imbedded in the form of the image itself.

To get a sense of these basic elements, I'd like to take you through a process I facilitated with grade twelve students in a downtown Toronto high school. After covering some of the economics of rock video, I established that my purpose was to talk about violence and sexuality in rock videos. I told them I was going to show a rock video and wanted them to help me analyze its contents. The video I chose was by the heavy metal band Mötley Crüe.

I asked the students to consider what was going on in the video, to count the number of violent acts, to notice who were the perpetrators and who were the victims, to watch for what women were doing in the scenario — were they active or were they just standing there? — and finally, to discuss why leather clothes were so important to the scene. The students went at it enthusiastically. It helped that heavy metal is an extremely popular target and that there were no heavy metal fans in the room (and be warned, this is not always the case). In fact I detected scorn for the boys and their guitars and this helped. Nobody felt threatened or personally criticized while the exercise was

taking place. In the end the class agreed that the video depicted a large number of violent acts; that women were often,
though not always, the victim; that men were invariably the
perpetrators; and that the women tended to just stand —
there the word *object* came from the students. About the
virtues of leather, the class was unclear. In classes of university
students I might have pressed for a discussion of the iconogra-
phy of sadomasochism, but without cues from the high school
students themselves I was not prepared to push it. In all, the
content analysis was very effective. The students began to see
how media images often harp on sex roles and stereotypes and
allowed that they didn't like the tendency much.

For the next step I showed another video, this time from
rhythm and blues singer Gregory Abbott. The song "Shake
You Down" describes what the singer anticipates will be a tor-
rid sexual encounter with his date. This example was appropriate because the song was at one point number one on the
charts and I knew the students would recognize it.

The video features Abbott languishing against a wall during his reverie while the camera surveys his date preparing for
the evening. The class was slightly baffled. Based on the first
step of the exercise, there was nothing to criticize in the
video. There were no overt acts of violence, no leather, no
ugly vibrations. We embarked on a deeper analysis. What role
was the camera playing? One student used the term *Peeping
Tom* to describe the camera's invasion of a woman's bedroom.
This was a breakthrough: realizing the camera acts as a voyeur
and that sometimes film situations are set up as an excuse to
watch women.

Soon we were comparing the portrayals of the man and
the woman. Though the singer was extremely handsome, and
thus to some extent himself an object, the video still depicted
his point of view, him imagining her. The class also noticed
that although this sexual encounter contained some elements
of equality, we never saw the man with his clothes off, only

the woman. Through this deconstruction process, the students discovered a more complex analysis of form and the camera's point of view.

To end the session I showed the class a video featuring Bruce Springsteen singing a song called "Fire." Springsteen, until recently, refused to be involved in any rock video. Finally his record company convinced him to do one or two but he insisted they be videos of live performances. "Fire" is one of these videos and features the singer/songwriter, wearing a white T-shirt and jeans, seated on a stool playing guitar for his ecstatic fans. The video ended and the class looked at me suspiciously. What was going on? No violence, not even any of the more subtle objectification strategies.

Yes, but what are the words, I wanted to know, returning to the basic question of content. One of the boys sprang up and recited: "I'm driving my car/You turn on the radio/I'm holding you close/You just say no/You say you don't like it but I know you're a liar/cause when we kiss fire."

"So what is happening here?" I asked. "He's raping her," came the reply. I had not expected the answer to come so quickly. "Really?" I said. "No means no," called out one girl. "Yes means maybe," said another boy, and the class laughed.

I was in an unusual situation. This ought to have been much harder and taken much longer. In another class the divisions by gender might be deeper or more hostile. What was different about this class was that it had done serious work on the issue of sexual violence. I found out later that one of the teachers at the school had done a session on date rape with the same class during sexual violence awareness week. The combination of that kind of sex education and my media strategies had made it easier for them to put things together. These students were part of a success story.

◆

I've found that after walking out of media and sexuality sessions in the classroom, I actually imagine that our work in the area of violence against women will become less of a mop-up operation. After years of wondering whether that could ever be, I can now envision a time when there will be no more victims, no more perpetrators, no market for pornography, no more lies about how women need force in sex, no more belief in the notion that unless men are violent, they are not men.

Femme Hy Hits New Low

Television advertising offers a rich area for studying the sensitive relationships between viewer desires, industry pressures and network responsibilities. A consistently contested terrain is one related to the marketing of products connected to sexuality, everything from condoms to tampons.

In 1982, I grew especially interested in television advertising after the tampon industry was rocked by Toxic Shock Syndrome, a life-threatening condition experienced by women who leave tampons inside themselves for too long. I wanted to know what the industry was going to do to get back consumer confidence. I discovered that many barriers had dropped during the eighties regarding the presentation of sex on prime time TV, making everyone wonder what they'd show next. But at the same time, ads for tampons, sanitary napkins and other feminine hygiene products were noteworthy for what they didn't show.

TELEVISION ADVERTISING has always had a hard time with the messy facts of life. The industry — dependent as it is on consumer insecurities — delivers an ideal image that doesn't mesh too well with the fact that bodies sweat and smell.

It has been particularly difficult for the medium to deal with the truth that women between the ages of twelve to fifty

---

Originally published in *Broadside*, July 1981.

go through a monthly hormonal change for which there are probably more euphemisms than there are for the part of the anatomy affected. And as ads continue to portray women as housewives or as adjuncts to cars and to men's colognes, we can't get any information about sexuality, our health or our bodies — even to sell a product — without causing hysteria in reactionary quarters. There is a vocal part of the public that has protested vigorously against feminine hygiene ads on television, or 'femme hy' as it is called in the trade. As a result, regulations have been changed in Canada so that on TV we are finding out less about tampons rather than more, Toxic Shock Syndrome be damned.

Before 1972, femme hy ads were not much of a phenomenon. Kotex and Tampax virtually dominated the market and large-scale TV ad campaigns, costly as they are — perhaps $90,000 for a 26-week contract — are not much use to monopolies. Since 1972, however, the market has been glutted with new femme hy products that do away with belts and uncomfortable paraphernalia or come with plastic applicators or can be scented and, naturally, the new products have spawned an array of TV ads designed to give women the good news.

Suddenly there was a little truth-telling going on. Products with names like Light Days came dangerously close to suggesting that there is such a thing as a flow that ebbs; the words *accident* and *spotting* crept into the copy in aggressive campaigns that were a far cry from the treacly Kotex ad that Kimberly-Clark had devised: fully animated butterflies flitting around a box of Kotex embedded in flowers. Inside the box there was — well gee, what *was* inside the box?

The fact is that certain consumer groups are determined to keep women as sheltered as ever. Nicole Parton, consumer columnist for the *Vancouver Sun*, spearheaded a coupon drive to get femme hy ads off the tube. The CRTC received thousands of these coupons, which bore the complaint that the ads were "invading viewer privacy [*sic*]."

While tampon and napkin advertisers cheerfully sang the praises of their new and improved products, the conservative contingent dreaded being caught watching television with their children when any of these ads came on. Without control over when these 'offensive' ads would hit the screen, they were faced with a situation where kids were asking questions and parents were forced to have conversations with their children that they didn't want to have.

In response to the public outcry, the CBC refused to carry any femme hy ads and the Canadian Association of Broadcasters (CAB) revised its code of standards in 1979. The code now demands that femme hy ads be pre-cleared with the Advertising Standards Council, the industry's watchdog, and that ads must 'keep the sensitivities of viewers in mind.' Whether an ad does so is still left for the licensed broadcaster to decide, but other new guidelines are not as open for interpretation.

For example, no ad, whether for a femme hy product or for a household cleaner, can 'play on fears.'

So, consider this ad's hypothetical narrative: a woman sitting in her summer whites appears to go into a panic. She runs over to a female friend and in dismayed but discreet tones confides that she's had a 'surprise.' "You should use Go with the Flow," her friend urges, and by happy coincidence is able to produce a sample from her handbag. She takes her friend on a guided tour of the tampon. "It's reliable, absorbent, keeps you fresh and it has a great new applicator for comfort."

This ad would give the Advertising Standards Council cardiac arrest. It breaks every rule in the book. To begin with the woman is dressed in white and so the ad plays on fears. That's not allowed. You can make everyone look impossibly thin, beautiful and wealthy to make consumers feel inadequate, but the ad can't put someone in personally embarrassing situations for which the product provides an escape. Accordingly, you'll never again see those unsightly flakes of dandruff that gross people out enough to convince you to buy dandruff shampoos. The American ad for Odor Eaters that features a shoe salesman falling into a dead faint when a customer removes his shoes will never be seen on Canadian television. And of course, it's good-bye to jungle mouth. Those ads play on fears.

Words like *surprise*, as well as *accidents* and *spotting*, are verboten because they make veiled reference to the fact that the unspeakable fluid has colour. Says Helen Murphy of the CRTC: "There was a groundswell of opinion that objected to the use of the words *spotting* or anything that suggested that women bleed once a month." (In the United States, by the way, any reference to the 'fluid' is a no-no and a tampon cannot be 'absorbent.' It must 'do what a tampon is supposed to do.') An ad for Playtex tampons that showed an exchange between two women did not pass by the Advertising Council's watchful eye because the use of the pronoun *you* made the ad 'too personalized.'

According to the new guidelines you cannot show the feminine hygiene product, so you can forget the guided tour of Go with the Flow. For that matter, if you insist on calling the product Go with the Flow, you will never get a TV slot because the name itself gives away the nature of a bodily function not fit for television. And since the CAB says that an ad cannot "employ graphic details of the product or the product's capabilities," any dialogue about applicators would have to be tossed out.

It's not the same for an underarm deodorant ad which can rattle on about a deodorant's roll-on or dry spray comfort for the full thirty seconds of ad time. You can stick whatever you like under your arms, but the CAB does not afford the same freedom when it comes to the area below the navel.

Femme hy ads appear on television only in the afternoon before four o'clock and in the evening after nine. This creates the cluster effect that allows you to view a wide range of femme hy commercials in a short time. Cathy Rigby swings on the parallel bars in an ad for Johnson & Johnson's Stayfree Maxi-pads. This is one in a series of ads for feminine hygiene products that suggests that if a woman works out in the gym, or (as in past campaigns) swims twelve laps, rides horses for hours, or plays seven games of tennis, she needs the special protection the advertised product can provide. Many women who are not up to this kind of activity at any time of the month find this selling technique hilarious, but it meets the standards and that's what counts. Brenda Vacarro huskily explains that Playtex believes every woman should use feminine hygiene products intelligently in a veiled reference to Toxic Shock Syndrome and the scandal that rocked the feminine hygiene industry. During the scare women seemed to talk of little else, but CAB and the rest of the bureaucracy couldn't quite bring themselves to accept the fact that the issue touches 53 percent of the population. In any event, the Playtex ad is about as direct as the advertising industry will allow.

In another commercial slot, you may see Scott Paper's exercise in the art of fence-sitting. When the conservative's vocal minority called for the removal of femme hy ads from television, much of the protest was generated in the west of Canada, where Scott Paper has its headquarters. Scott dutifully pulled its ads for Confidets sanitary napkins off the air. But with its share of the market 'stagnant' and Scott's Confidets now new and improved, Scott wanted back in the TV ad arena. Question: How to do it without really doing it? Answer: Do it but insist you're not. A woman enters a set decorated with plastic greenery and a floral patterned sofa. The woman is carrying magazines. "We at Scott Paper," she begins, "believe that there are certain products you don't want to hear about on television," whereupon we are invited to learn about Scott's new improved product by reading its magazine advertisements. Translation: Here we are on television, paying thousands of dollars for the privilege, telling you why we're not on television.

All of this demure nonsense is the result of a conservative backlash that hasn't uttered a sound about exploitation. An ad for a safety razor makes the sniggering point that "you don't have to get wet to get close." Models cosy up to each other in a celebration of the sexual rewards that accrue to wearing the right designer jeans. Sexy is 'in,' sexual is 'out.' You can turn a woman into an object but don't articulate her bodily needs.

Update 1995

In the past twelve years the Advertising Standards Code administered by the Canadian Advertising Foundation has undergone three evolutions, each of which has significantly loosened restrictions on tampon ads. Femme hy ads may now appear on weekdays during the afternoon soap slots and in prime time before 9:00 pm. Ads may also now refer to light days and heavy days and to the individual benefits of the product. But references to accidents or bleeding are still not acceptable and playing on fears is forbidden, as it continues to be with all products advertised on television.

Still, signs that the culture has not shed its fear of female bodies rose in the most unlikely place when the Women's Tennis Association turned down a sponsorship bid from the makers of Tampax.

What wildness is going on in the women's tennis circuit these days? The Women's Tennis Association has just turned down a $10-million sponsorship bid from Tampax, claiming

---

Originally published as "Women's Bodies Too Much For TV," in
NOW magazine, February 23-29, 1995.

that sidling up to a 'feminine hygiene' product would turn off other potential partners.

Listening to Martina Navratilova, president of the association and one of the world's most famous out lesbians, trying to explain the commercial value of the latest conservative cave-in is a surreal sensation. You'd think that women's tennis would get behind a reliable tampon. Players do have to wear white on the court — no matter what time of the month it is.

The association isn't the only organization queasy about anything associated with the fact that women menstruate. Advertising standards for feminine hygiene products are very specific. Playing on fears is not allowed, and that has been interpreted in the case of television ads to mean that an ad can only allude to the particular function of a pad or tampon, though you can mention what benefits each product has. That means you can talk about the wings, but saying what they're for won't fly.

The upshot in the case of femme hy ads makes for some misleading messages. I mean, when all is said and done, what's on sale here?

It all reminds me of the three prepubescent boys who come across a five dollar bill on the street. What should they do with it, they wonder.

"Let's go share a burger and fries," says the first one. "I'm starved."

"No, let's go to the video arcade," says the second. "We could settle in for hours."

"No way. Let's buy a box of Tampax," said the third. "Then we can go swimming, horseback riding, play tennis ...."

Women's tennis, take note.

ABUSIVE AMUSEMENT

Though popular culture, which reinvents itself and finds new high-tech vehicles of expression every day, is the most dynamic subject for the debate on images and violence the high end of the cultural spectrum is also an intriguing target for critical analysis. Just because a work is a piece of art does not, in my mind, make it any less vulnerable to hard thought. The subject of Boucher's nudes were the mistresses of Louis XV, for example, and the king hung the portraits in his chambers in order to display his sexual prowess. To be painted was to be owned. To be exhibited was to be advertised. Virtuosity of execution in a work of art does not make it any less pornographic or worthy of critical scrutiny. What follows is a review of two theatre classics that winds up wondering whether classical narratives featuring violence against women are fit for the contemporary stage.

SITTING AT THE Festival Theatre in Stratford, Ontario, I found myself watching *My Fair Lady* with deep ambivalence. The production values were superb, as is usually the case with Canada's most prestigious drama festival, the music familiar, the ways the thrust stage was used as a venue for musical theatre, ingenious.

But the story itself is fraught with political problems.

From *Broadside*, November 1988.

Henry Higgins bets he can pass off the flower girl Eliza as a duchess at the next Embassy Ball. All he needs is six months to work on her speech problems and to clean up her manners. During the course of her tutelage he submits her to all manner of abuses, including verbal assault, starvation and sleep deprivation. All of this is contextualized — and invariably interpreted by audiences — as diverting amusements followed by the happy ending in which, after bolting from Higgins's household, Eliza returns, presumably to take up a romantic relationship with her tormentor.

At the same time, the Stratford Festival has mounted a wildly inventive production of Shakespeare's ode to female oppression, *The Taming of the Shrew*. Here the theme of female makeover at the hands of a tyrannical male is played to the hilt as Petruchio tames Kate with many of the same tactics as Higgins has used to cow Eliza. There are differences, of course. Petruchio triumphs over Kate, turning her into the 'perfect' submissive wife (boy wins girl and keeps her) whereas Higgins loses Eliza and then gets her back (boy, or rather man, wins girl, loses her and then gets her back). But either way, the plays bring up the thorny problem of whether major theatre companies ought to bother with revivals of obnoxiously unenlightened works.

My Fair Lady is based on George Bernard Shaw's play *Pygmalion* and certainly the socialist and cynic cannot be blamed for the regressive romanticism of the 1950s musical comedy Lerner and Loewe fashioned out of this play. The play's title refers to the myth in which the misogynist artist Pygmalion sculpts what he thinks is the perfect woman, only to fall in love with the creation which, voiceless and immobile, can provide him with no emotional sustenance.

Interestingly enough, Shaw wrote his *Pygmalion* without the creator Higgins falling in love with his own artwork. The original play ends with Eliza leaving Higgins while the professor scoffs at the idea of Eliza marrying Freddie Eynsford-Hill.

Higgins may have wanted to continue to control Eliza, but he never wanted her as a lover. This may be inconsistent with the Pygmalion myth but it is perfectly consistent with Shaw's inveterate distaste for romantic relationships whether in his own life or among his plays' characters.

Not surprising, audiences were not very satisfied with the ending of *Pygmalion* but Shaw stuck to his guns and, as Stratford's excellent program notes detail, wrote at some length of why he ended his story there. The play's happy ending, he insisted, hinges on Eliza's escape from Higgins's tyranny, and if audiences wanted something else, they had missed the point. Shaw could not imagine a worse relationship than that between a middle-aged, middle-class man with a mother fixation and a nineteen-year-old flower girl. Better for Eliza to have found someone her own age who was crazy about her. A film version of *Pygmalion* made in the thirties created a romantic link between Higgins and Eliza, but Shaw never approved.

Imagine how outraged he would have been at Lerner and Loewe's version of the story. Browbeaten for six months and then ignored after she triumphs at the Embassy Ball, Eliza walks out on Higgins, goes out on a date with Freddy and then goes to visit Higgins's mother. The professor finds her there but when he implores her to return she tells him to go to hell. Ah, but not for long. As he edges up the path to his house he realizes that "he's grown accustomed to her face"; the audience melts and then thrills as Eliza arrives, gently switches off the tapes of her voice he has unearthed and announces that she's back. Higgins reverts immediately to his old ways, and the final line of the play, "Eliza, where the devil are my slippers?" does not augur well for equality.

Most everything about *My Fair Lady* —its commentary on language, class and morals — is Shaw's (two thirds of the book comes directly from the play), and what greatness is left, namely in the lyrics, is sorely wasted. The wit of "I'm an

Ordinary Man (Let a Woman in Your Life)" and "Why Can't a Woman be More like a Man?" both written to categorize Higgins as a staunch woman-hater, fades with the sentimental strategy of turning Higgins into a salvageable love object. The Stratford production, a faithful and gorgeous revival, does very little to reinterpret the work, leaving the play with its nagging problems.

To be fair, it would be tough to do anything else. *My Fair Lady* is time-specific, written to evoke the particular class conflicts of Edwardian England. But perhaps a company at some time will find a way to present the story's happy ending without evoking a wince from any self-respecting woman in the audience.

When it comes to the works of William Shakespeare, the dilemma is slightly different. Many feminists have insisted that *The Taming of the Shrew* should be shredded and never presented on our national stages. The story is viciously anti-woman and you could make the case that the central dynamic of the play creates pleasure in what amounts to violence against women. Scholars counter that Shakespeare was a product of his time and that nothing from the mind of the greatest English-language poet should be tossed aside; even with its egregious celebration of woman abuse, the play has redeeming social values.

This year's Stratford production presents another argument, namely that the works of Shakespeare can be reinterpreted in the light of what we know now so that the play can convey some meaning even to twentieth-century audiences. It's been done before. Franco Zefferelli's 1967 film version offered a conventional reading but audiences tended to be amused by what they thought was a metaphor for the passionate relationship between the two stars, Elizabeth Taylor and Richard Burton.

Another version of the *Shrew* presented in 1978 by the Royal Shakespeare Company in England was extremely self-conscious about the play's misogyny. Michael Bogdanov's production, done in modern dress, presented the taming of Kate, played by Daola Dionisetti, not as a comedy but as a horror show so grotesque that even Petruchio (Alun Armstrong) is repelled at the end by the submissive woman he has created. Dionisetti gives it an added twist — without Petruchio seeing, she winks at the audience.

This 1988 Stratford production does not tamper with the meaning of Shakespeare's text in the same way. Instead, it sets the play in the 1950s, the same repressive decade that spawned the musical *My Fair Lady*, so that the female oppression is placed in a completely different historical context. This is an inspired tragedy, for Shakespeare's male characters, with their preening and posturing and their unquestioned ownership of women, would have been right at home in the fifties. And the ingenue Bianca, presented as a blond bimbo reminiscent of the icon (not the person) Marilyn Monroe, would have been in her prime in that decade of saddle shoes, cashmere blouses and rise of the nuclear family. If you hate the text and subtext of *Taming of the Shrew*, you definitely hated the fifties. Director Richard Monette creates a neat marriage of the two.

But many women will tell you that the technical fireworks (literally, there's even a motorcycle on the set) and other clever ploys (Shakespeare's sonnets sung to Louis Applebaum's fifties rock score) cannot salvage the actual experience of having to watch Kate being abused by Petruchio. If you have an ounce of awareness of the real horror of wife assault, it is difficult to stomach it presented as a comic *divertissement*.

Yet according to the program (and this we have to face), *The Taming of the Shrew* is especially popular among female viewers. Why? Is it the classic fantasy of the tall dark stranger subduing the feisty female that is so appealing? Or are women so well socialized that they too find women being tortured a source of entertainment? The extent to which we identify more with what's bad for us than with what's good for us is rather sad testimony to how our tastes and bodies are colonized by the prevailing sexual values of male violence and female submission.

LOSING IT ON LESBIAN CHIC

WELCOME TO THE Gay Nineties. Are we having fun yet? We're supposed to be, now that gays and lesbians are officially chic. I have to say that I've been waiting for this to happen. It was just a matter of time before anyone with a tad of entrepreneurial sense or a nose for demographics figured out that gays and lesbians are a marketer's dream.

We share relatively high disposable incomes, fewer dependent children than straight couples and we share a value system — some would even say an aesthetic — that any marketing consultant can tap into with ease.

But homophobia has proven a powerful force, stronger even than the appeal of guaranteed profits. A writer friend of mine told me how she could not convince her publisher to mention gay aspects of her murder mystery on the back cover of a paperback, even though she could prove that such a strategy could guarantee sales to a sizeable and quantifiable market. The resistance to gay marketing reminds me of Gloria Steinem's astonishingly futile attempts to convince major car corporations to buy advertising space in the fledgling *Ms.* magazine. No amount of data detailing women's impact in the work force and their rising buying power could overcome General Motor's fear of feminism.

So, too, has Hollywood waited, hiding its homosexuals in a frenzy of panic that only an AIDS death to the likes of Rock

Originally published in *Herizons*, Winter 1994.

Hudson could expose, while we waited and grovelled for any shred of evidence that lesbians and gays existed. We, naturally, went out of our minds with delight if any of these media products presented lesbians as sexual and sexy. We have been desperate enough that a three-minute sequence featuring a three-second kiss on *L.A. Law* between a bisexual female and a confused heterosexual woman can cause a sensation among lesbians who had never seen such a thing on prime time TV.

Until now, that is. Now, they're coming out on TV, out on film, out on stage and, thanks to Canada's own k.d. lang, out on record and on the record.

When I saw lang grinning off the cover of *New York Magazine* and the headline blazing "Lesbian Chic," I was thrilled to the bone. This, I thought, is exactly what we need, something that promotes lesbian life. In high school classes, where I've done media literacy seminars on violence and sexuality, kids' consciousness of gay-positive anything is way behind even their sketchy understanding of male violence. Why shouldn't kids get the message that it's hip to be a lesbian?

My friends, especially those who, like me, work with kids, were not so sure. They worried that young people on the verge of coming out would be intimidated by the idea that they had to be beautiful to matter, or worse, that they wouldn't come out unless they fit into a conventional beauty mold. They also wondered whether gay and lesbian values were not being co-opted by media's attempt to make us look like just another groovy group to exploit, at the same time eviscerating our community's values to the point where we stopped looking like a force for social change. A word like *chic*, they said, is incompatible with a word like *radical.*

At the time, I thought this was preposterous, and typical of progressive groups' panic when something happens that might drag them out of the margins. The word *chic* does not cancel out the word *radical,* I thought. In fact the term *radical chic* was coined for the glitterati who threw trendy bashes in the sixties to fundraise for the Black Panthers or for Vietnam war resisters. Frankly, I don't think those activities should be disparaged. With any luck, I thought, coining the term *lesbian chic* might foster a few hip and happening — to say nothing about profitable — benefits for gay rights. I was doing fine with this perspective until I saw k.d. lang and Cindy Crawford mixing it up on the cover of *Vanity Fair* (November 1993) — and I mean mixing it up. I think it's a big stretch to interpret the image of a bearded k.d. lang getting it on with the bustier-bearing supermodel as a clever sabotage of patriarchal cultural norms. Really. There are exactly two entertainment mega-stars who have said publicly that they are lesbians — lang and Martina Navratilova. This means there is more invested in the visible choices they make. I wish lang were one of hundreds of lesbians who were public and proud so that it didn't matter if she was guilty of a lapse in taste or political judgment on the cover of *Vanity Fair*. But as it is, the visuals accompanying the image and the interview of the one lesbian household name in America makes it look like lesbians suffer from a terminal case of penis envy.

It also makes lesbian chic look like a politically bankrupt concept. I became more convinced of this when lesbian chic started hitting the talk shows. There's Geraldo gabbing away with the latest wave of open lesbians, and I start to wonder. These women have big hair. I've never seen so much big hair in my life. And I don't mean long hair, I mean big hair. The way things are going, lesbian chic is starting to mean looking the way heterosexual women look when they want to please men. Then before I could chastise myself for being judgemental, one of the guests said, "I want to be able to have long hair and wear high heels and walk into a lesbian bar without feeling like I don't fit in."

Is this what we're fighting for — the right to wear restrictive clothing? To spend whatever disposable income we have on cosmetics? To be sexual objects and to sexually objectify others? Maybe lesbian chic is not enough because lesbian politics don't make for meaningful change without a hit of feminism. I think that's it. What we really need is lesbian-feminist chic.

V

VIOLENCE

Home Sweet Home?

At first we called it 'wife battery.' At the time "Home Sweet Home" was written, in 1982, we called it 'wife assault' to emphasize that the behaviour was illegal. Uncomfortable with the use of the marital term 'wife assault,' we tried using the term 'spousal assault' only to discover that we were missing the point if we couldn't use a term that reflected the reality of who is doing what to whom. Now we call it 'violence against women in the home,' making sure that we encompass the entire spectrum of abuse.

But other things have not changed. An individual woman who is being abused needs to know she is not alone. All of us need to know the pervasiveness of 'intimate' violence that is part of many women's lives. Along with rape, violent pornography and sexual harassment, 'wife battering' forms the web that keeps us in our place. And whereas statistics told us in 1982 that one in ten women living with her spouse is beaten by him, we know now that the figure is more like one in eight.

IF WE TAKE THE avid advertiser at his word, the home is a happy haven, a place where all that has to be toughed out is a little ring around the collar. Right-wingers, particularly of late, have hammered away at the old line. They insist that the nuclear family is the last hope for keeping us all civilized, the

From *Still Ain't Satisfied! Canadian Feminism Today*, M. Fitzgerald, C. Guberman and M. Wolfe, eds. Toronto: The Women's Press, 1982.

institution that is guaranteed to keep male carnality under control.

It isn't working that way though, and evidently, male brutality is not easily contained. Within the family, within this much-touted paradise, one out of every ten women is staggering. She is nursing broken bones and tending the bruises that are the result of assault at the hand of her husband or live-in partner. No fact smashes the myth of the happy family more than the one that estimates that 24,000 women in Canada are battered wives. The extent of the damage goes beyond the use of profanity or the occasional slap of the hand. It means cracked ribs, concussions and miscarriages, the result of being kicked in the belly while pregnant. Over ten percent of the homicide victims in Canada are women murdered by their husbands. The facts tell us that the words *home, sweet home* are the fabrication either of a deluded fabulist or a skilled propagandist.

Two years ago, Margaret Campbell, then MPP for the district of St. George in Ontario, delivered this nasty truth to her colleagues in the Legislature. She was particularly interested in taking the Attorney General of Ontario, Roy McMurtry, to task. Why were there no more women's shelters? Why were police refusing to lay assault charges on spouses who were beating their wives? Why did it all keep going on?

McMurtry, at the time a crusader preoccupied with laying assault charges on hockey players who couldn't keep their sticks down, hadn't thought a good deal about wife assault. He had known that the subject would come up on the floor and yet he sputtered and groped for words. Then, out of his mouth (and chronicled by the legislative record), came the ingenuous confession: "People become so frustrated and disturbed with their lot in life, that they will lash out at society in general, and, for some peculiar reasons better understood by psychiatrists and psychologists than by lawyers, they tend often to use people of whom they should again be most protective as the most convenient target."

Lawmakers, especially those who stand for election, are inclined to mince words. Campbell's question concerned the assault of women at the hands of men and yet McMurtry insists on talking about the assailants as 'people.' He wonders why these 'people' go after the most vulnerable targets. Women, after all, belong on the pedestal, not on the other end of someone's fists.

And so the attorney general would like to know why men beat their wives. Psychologists and psychiatrists, in spite of the confidence he's given them, have not discovered the reasons. It's been left to women — feminists, mostly — to grapple with the question. As it turns out, the answer is not 'peculiar' at all, but rather is devastatingly simple. Men beat their wives because they are permitted to do so. And although, technically speaking, wife assault is no longer legal, there is enough strong cultural reinforcement of it to ensure that the assault will continue.

Every time a psychologist or a social worker tells a woman that she should be less 'dominating' and try not to provoke the beatings, the counsellor places the blame on the victim and gives her husband an excuse for battering away. The victim is accused of having violated sex-role stereotypes and the husband is given carte blanche to punish her for her crime. The social working establishment's commitment to the preservation of the nuclear family has made it possible for the family to become a convenient arena for men to exercise total power.

Every time a wife batterer consumes pornographic material, an estimated 50 percent of which depicts women as the willing victims of violence, he is given cultural reinforcement and permission for the assault. He is reminded that women are objects to be seen and not heard, voiceless receptacles for his sexual pleasure or for release of his own violent tension.

Pornography, as it plays its role as propaganda for male domination, tells the wife beater that his actions are appropriate, sometimes even to be celebrated.

Every time a police officer refuses to interfere in a domestic quarrel ('domestic' is another term used to disguise that it is usually women who are victimized by men), the officer gives permission to the assailant to continue the attack. This refusal by the police to get involved has been an ongoing travesty of law enforcement. At worst, male officers, otherwise quite comfortable with breaking down the doors of private houses, suddenly become protective of the family's privacy when the crime is wife assault. At best, the police agree to walk the assailant around the block to cool him off. Seldom do the police press assault charges and then only when they have witnessed the attack.

A February 1982 ruling by the Supreme Court of Canada has made it impossible for the victims of wife assault to secure restraining orders from family court judges. Now they must go right to the Supreme Court in order to get protection in their homes from violent husbands. The cost and length of time required to secure orders have escalated to the point that women are waiting weeks and spending much more money than previously on legal advice in order to secure protection. The courts have betrayed women in other ways, for example, by not letting an assault charge stick in many cases. Every assault charge finally pressed that does not result in conviction gives more permission to the wife batterer to carry on as he has. As the police and the courts continue to be lenient, the wife beater is convinced that the home is truly his castle and that no one, not even the uniformed cop or the robed judge, will brook his authority.

But let the McMurtrys of the world ask their naive questions. Those of us aware of the power of sexism and the prerogative given in a sexist society to brute force and male privilege know full well why men beat their wives and get away with it.

As long as the media deliver their barrage of images of women as objects, as long as failure to comply with strict sex-role stereotypes is deemed a punishable offence and men are allowed to minister the punishment, as long as the police want to steer clear, as long as sexism is alive and well in our society, men will continue to beat their wives.

What we can't understand is why a battered woman would stay in her situation for more. In fact, she doesn't go back for more. Saying so assumes that she is giving permission to men to assault her. This is the single most important assumption to dispel.

The popular myth has it that the typical battered woman has a masochistic pathology, that she is a strange and different freak when, actually, she isn't an anomaly at all. She is isolated in the home, usually with children, always with the desperate wish that her marriage work. Invariably she is imbued with any number of romantic notions, that love conquers all, for example, and that the best way to make the conquest is within the framework of traditional sex roles. The first assault is likely to be verbal and will take her totally by surprise. The attacks will escalate in ferocity — from a slap, to a slam, to a pummel.

But she has absorbed the myths of the family well, even if her own experience belies these myths. One out of four battered women experienced violence as a child. Far from being convinced that family life is lacking, she assumes that violence is a part of the family package deal. Marriage is her only lot in life, or so she thinks. If cuts and bruises go with it, so be it. And the scrapes and broken bones aren't so bad, especially when compared with the tenderness she receives after the attack. Wife batterers tend to do that, to be achingly kind and, apparently, sincerely contrite after the worst is over. These men don't exist in their wives' eyes as animals. They are fathers, lovers, friends. The violent side of them is perceived by the battered as the sad exception, something that can change and get better even though the attacks inevitably grow more intense with each incident.

Since the propaganda from media, from every institution including the church, relentlessly preaches the virtues of family life, a woman whose life in the home is a violent nightmare believes that she must be doing something wrong. Is the food too well cooked? Is the table too dusty? Am I giving enough? Do I love him enough?

Even if she is able to place the blame somewhere else, she is convinced that the problem is her own. She is alone. She would be shocked to discover that her life is not atypical at all, that there are thousands of others going through the same turmoil, that her experience is a graphic reflection of the sexism every woman confronts.

She may get an inkling that she needs help and will go to a social worker. He or she might chide her for complaining about a perfectly normal situation and she will feel foolish. Sometimes she never gets the urge to seek help again. A variety of incidents may trigger the radical action of leaving home. Often the choice to leave occurs to her only when she's been hospitalized after an attack. Many times she thinks to flee only when her husband threatens her children.

This woman could come from any income bracket. She is as likely to be the wife of a professional architect as she is to be the spouse of a manual worker or of someone unemployed. Wife battery as a phenomenon crosses class lines and compels us to view women as a 'class' dominated by specific social forces and restraints.

Chances are, for example, the wife of the upwardly mobile executive will have an encounter with a psychiatrist similar to the one the working-class woman has with a social worker. No matter the family income, the victim of wife assault shies away from relatives and friends who must not learn what she believes to be true — that she is a failure. Regardless of economic class background, the battered woman is usually dependent on her husband for funds and has no personal income to dispense. If the wealthier woman has access to a credit card, she may go to a hotel, but only for temporary shelter. For the most part, up until ten years ago, if a battered woman, even in spite of her intense socialization, was able to get to the point where she knew she had to get out, there was nowhere to go.

The first short-term solution to the problem of wife battery thus became shelter. The founders of Interval House in Toronto had a partial handle on the situation. They wanted to create a hostel, a place where women could come if they wanted out of a restrictive marriage or if they were in crises that forced them to move suddenly.

"It wasn't until the hostel was opened that we realized that women were running away from dangerous situations," confessed Trudy Don, coordinator of women's shelters in Ontario. "We became aware as soon as the phone started to ring." It did not take long for the hostel to become a shelter for battered women.

Of course, a culture that permits wife battery is not likely to foster governments that will provide the means to rectify the situation. Jillian Ridington succinctly explained why in her article on the transition houses started in Vancouver in 1970: "Setting up an institution for the specific purposes of aiding battered wives," she writes, "implies that the problem is not only widespread but that it is a social problem rather than an individual one. It also implies ... that women have the right to leave the men who abuse them."[1]

No wonder then that the shelter movement grew out of the non-traditional grassroots women's movement. It took clear-headed feminist thinking to devise a comprehensive analysis and a strategy to separate the government from some of its money. It helped considerably that the government in the early 1970s was given to doling out grants, part of its strategy to mollify rowdy radicals. Yet dependence on the state for funding has come back to haunt the shelter movements. Now that the state is much less generous, coordinators of shelters across the country yearn for more stable funding so they will not have to spend so much time looking for funds.

In 10 years, 75 shelters have sprung up across the country, making available to battered women approximately 700 beds — for 24,000 physically abused women. The numbers speak eloquently for the desperate need for more shelters.

Ideally, providing shelter for the battered wife is the first stage in her transition from dependent and battered to independent and secure. The shelters provide a woman with support. The workers inside describe to her the options and make the connections with welfare officers who can provide funds and a more permanent roof over the woman's head. Most important, the battered woman discovers that she is not alone.

"The transition house," writes Jillian Ridington, "facilitates the process of examination and reconceptualization by providing a social context in which alternative ideologies and behaviours are necessary and workable; a milieu in which women see other women acting authoritatively, believing independently while making decisions."[2] But the seemingly ideal environment of the shelter can be enormously alienating for a typical victim of wife abuse.

Out of her isolation she is plunged into a cooperative setting, a noisy one, with little privacy. For non-natives of Canada, the problem is exacerbated when few or none of the people inside the shelter speak her language. And while we may assume that seeing women acting authoritatively would leave a salutary effect on a woman whose self-esteem is low, it can work the other way around. Many women seeking shelter have never really talked to women at all and think the exercise is useless. It's men's approval they are after.

Encouraged, and rightly so, to find economic independence, a battered wife throws herself onto a job market that is not hospitable to women and shows no signs of becoming so. In her frustration she turns to the welfare officer, who tells her that as a woman with two children she can receive $258 a month in benefits. She discovers that she cannot rent a room for less than $50 a week, which leaves her with $58 to take care of herself and her children.

Suddenly the prospect of an independent life does not seem so appealing and her former situation does not seem so bad. She doesn't want to be alone. She already has a home, her own possessions and a life that she believes belongs to her. Besides, many women come to a shelter for temporary relief only, to keep away from their husbands until the storm has passed. Yet we ask battered women to realize the necessity and desirability of making changes in their lives. Given the restrictions on staying periods in shelters, is it reasonable to expect them to make the changes in less than a month? More often than not, the battered wife does return home. The horror of her experience is underscored by the agony of the shelter worker who cannot work miracles, who can only grant the victim the right to choose and who must watch as a woman goes back home, possibly to be maimed for life. The battered woman returns three or four times before she decides that she can change her life.

If the victim of wife assault has to transform before she can emerge, our whole society has to be shaken to its roots in order for wife beating to cease. In the face of it all, it is amazing that workers in the field have not thrown up their hands in despair and resignation.

But they haven't, largely because they have placed the issue in its historical context. Wife battery has been a fact of women's lives for thousands of years. A movement ten years old is unlikely to stem the tide of centuries of approval for men who beat up women.

As is the case with most feminist issues, women are working on all fronts. The short term has the priority, more so with the issue of wife assault than with some other feminist endeavours. Women's lives, after all, are literally at stake.

Shelter workers, sociologists and social workers agree that if we can't create a wholesale change in attitudes, we can at least affect the behaviour of people who come in contact with battered women. The campaign is being waged on two fronts specifically — within the legal system and among social workers in traditional agencies.

Roundly criticized for shrugging off domestic squabbles as incidents 'outside of their jurisdiction,' police have set up domestic response teams around the country, some of which combine the authority of the police with the service of social workers. Like any police initiative, the emergence of these teams can easily be viewed cynically. The motivation for the projects was the safety of police officers, not the safety of women. Police departments realized that 50 percent of their domestic calls involved wife abuse and that the lives of policemen were endangered when they were trying to drag assailants away from their victims. There are now seven teams across the country, in Restigouche, Toronto, Hamilton, London, Edmonton, Vancouver and Surrey.

Recent studies of the criminal justice system reveal that the courts and police are ambivalent about their dealings with wife abuse and, accordingly, have perpetuated the victim's cycle of helplessness. In London, for example, police refused to lay charges except in 4 percent of the cases they dealt with. Out of 40 cases in which women were advised to get medical treatment, only 6 charges were laid. Of 56 cases that went to court, only 23 defendants were found guilty and only 4 went to jail — all this in spite of the fact that the study showed that women were twice as likely to get assaulted again if charges were not laid.

The justice system has a long way to go, but the domestic response teams still serve three crucial functions. First, they give us a sense of what is going on out there. Toronto's domestic response team expanded into a new division and the number of reports of wife abuse tripled within a month. Police teams are helping to provide useful statistics that more accurately reflect how widespread wife battery really is.

Second, the social workers who accompany the police explain to the victim her choices, that there is shelter, that there are people she can talk to. The workers follow through by accompanying the woman to a shelter if that is where she wants to go or by setting up interviews with other social workers.

Third, the policeman himself — or herself for that matter; apparently assailants become quite calm at the sight of a female officer — makes it plain to the attacker that what he is doing is against the law. To wife batterers who have flailed away with impunity in the past, this is important information. Now all that's left is for the police to put their real clout where their mouths are and actually press the charges they threaten to lay.

Practically every former victim of wife abuse has a horror story about a social worker or a psychiatrist who has blamed her for her plight. One of the vital components of a domestic violence project operating in Toronto is the education of professionals who have day-to-day dealings with battered women and who, in the past, have not been able to give them meaningful assistance. Their failure has to do with the fact that social workers too have been overrun with the myths that surround the phenomenon of wife assault.

Deborah Sinclair and Susan Harris travel the country to lead workshops designed to bring the consciousness of the non-traditional shelter movement into the traditional agencies. At these workshops, Harris and Sinclair attempt to turn people's thinking around. They make it plain that no woman likes to be abused; that the extent of the crime is greatly underestimated; that alcohol consumption doesn't cause violence against women, it excuses it; that women do not provoke the attacks but are sometimes even dragged from their beds to be beaten; that the victims of wife assault are not masochistic, but rather are resigned to their situations; that men should be made responsible for stopping their violent behaviour and that the sole responsibility of women is not to accept victim status; that the hearth is not so happy and that any social worker who encourages a woman to return to the bosom of the nuclear family and the institution of marriage may be sending a woman to her death. This last point is not rhetoric or hyperbole. Sixty percent of female homicide victims between the years 1961 and 1974 were murdered in the family context. Harris and Sinclair are among a handful doing this kind of work and they are making huge inroads, given their small numbers.

Every shelter that has been opened in Canada over the past ten years has been filled within a week. That is not so surprising. If there were 1,000 shelters instead of just 75, they would be crammed just as quickly. The need for more shelters is painfully obvious. Women working inside are absorbed with dealing with the immediate crises of the women who come to them and it has been difficult to muster a full-scale campaign to get more government funding for transition houses.

Still, there has been a flicker of interest in government circles. The Canadian Advisory Council on the Status of Women funded a Canada-wide study of wife assault and the result is Linda MacLeod's fine overview entitled *Wife Battering in Canada*. The information in the study galvanized the research division of the federal government to produce more studies, one on service to victims of crime in Canada and another on the social service role of police in domestic crisis intervention. The danger, as usual, is that wife battery will be studied to death. The federal Parliament, giving the impression that it had some interest in the matter, established an all-party committee that invited briefs and testimonies addressing the question of domestic violence and shelter. A total of twelve people have spoken to the committee. Three politicians, a male psychiatrist and a male legal expert, both sympathetic to the needs of abused women, are among them. Only three people working in the front lines of the shelters have made an appearance in front of the committee. There is fear that the committee will be useful only to those who want to make political hay out of the issue.

Worse still, if the issue isn't studied to death, it may be talked to death. But Trudy Don, one of the founders of Interval House in Toronto, is insisting that the front-line workers be heard. They are the ones who will cut through the verbiage. They are the ones who can state the truth succinctly — that there is simply not enough shelter for battered women, that 700 beds are not meeting the needs of 24,000 women who, if given the chance, could stagger away from their nightmare.

In May 1982, Margaret Mitchell (NDP, Vancouver) asked the House of Commons the same question Margaret Campbell demanded of Roy McMurtry in Ontario two years earlier. Why were there no more shelters? But the honourable members did not take the query seriously enough even to deliver the kinds of platitudes Ontario's Roy McMurtry had been able to muster. Instead, a ripple of laughter was heard, and from all sides of the House. No other single incident in parliamentary history so vividly conveys how firmly entrenched sexism is in Canada.

A furious response from women across the country forced an apology from the House to all Canadian women. Members of Parliament, in a fit of mortification, may move faster now than they would have had the parliamentary wheels been left to their customary slow churn. But even if the all-party committee were to recommend to Parliament that legislation be enacted granting millions of dollars to shelters across the country, and even if members of parliament could stop sniggering long enough to take such action, we would only have put battered women on the mend. We will not have put an end to the beatings. Until sex roles are eliminated, until the family no longer serves as that convenient arena for male violence, until wife beating is no longer a logical extension of male domination — in other words, as long as sexism exists, the beatings will continue.

The eradication of sexism, of course, is no simple task and there is no simple blueprint for change. But two main areas have to be addressed. The first, naturally, is education, not only education within the legal system and traditional family agencies as they've been described here, but education within the classroom as well. One thing we know for certain is that men learn their privilege when they are young and women absorb the propaganda designed to keep them down at an equally early age. Unless young people are infused with a new set of values, the patterns of wife assault are bound to repeat themselves.

Second, the silence that surrounds wife battery has to be broken. The violence perpetrated against women in our culture is something that is not talked about often enough. And so, the activities of women organizing against violence against women take on a new significance. The act of political demonstration seeks to convey to the public the notion that violence is not a fantasy confined to the pages of a pornographic magazine and that women are angry about it. Of even greater import is the message this kind of high-profile political protest gives to women who are the victims of violence in the home. By emphasizing the pervasiveness of violence against women in our society, we tell women that they are not alone, that they are not the ones to blame and that they have support.

But none of us can be effective until we dispense with the baggage that clutters up our own view of the battered woman herself. The battered woman is not a testament to the frailty of women but to the power of sexism.

Update 1995

Linda MacLeod was able to update her groundbreaking study *Wife Battering in Canada* and in 1990 reported that now one in eight women living with their spouses is being abused by him. In the meantime, the Canadian Advisory Council on the Status of Women, which funded this and other breakthrough research, is now defunct thanks to its dismantling at the hands of the Liberal government in 1995.

Stats Can 1993 reports that 29 percent of the 2.7 million women who had ever been married or lived common law had been physically or sexually assaulted by their partner. Note that this refers only to women who are in live-in situations and only refers to incidents chargeable under the criminal code. Twenty-one percent were assaulted during pregnancy and 40 percent of that figure stated that the abuse started when they were pregnant. Twenty percent reported that the abuse began during or after separation and 35 percent said that the violence increased in intensity during that time. Of the women who reported assault, 60 percent said the assaults were repeated, 41 percent more than 10 times, and a full 44 percent said that weapons were used against them.

Most disturbing is a new study undertaken by the Women We Honour action group entitled *Women Killing: Intimate Femicide in Ontario, 1974-1990*. The study indicates that 551 women were killed by their partners. Thirty-one percent were killed after they left and the study concludes that women separated from their partners were found to be at a particular risk. Now, when men tell women they'll kill them if they leave, we have reason to believe they will.

The *Report on Police Response to Incidents of Wife Abuse in Metro Toronto*, undertaken by the Metro Toronto Committee Against Wife Assault and the Assaulted Women's Help Line, tell the grim story of police inactivity in the area. Despite new protocols requiring officers to lay charges when an assault has taken place, not much has changed. Many women were hesitant to report to police because the situations were not taken seriously. In 1992, 55 percent of help-line callers said their calls were not taken seriously, 58 percent in 1993 and 63 percent in the first part of 1994. During that period, although 64 percent of calls reported an assault and 27 percent reported assault causing injury, police laid charges in only 58 percent of all cases.

Whereas in 1982 there were 75 shelters in Canada, there are now 75 shelters in Ontario alone and close to 280 shelters across the country. In Canada's largest province of Ontario, where for the past three years programs almost everywhere else were axed severely, political pressure and public awareness kept women's services intact. This is something that feminist activists can be proud of. We did win something — except that all over Canada the shelters, especially in urban areas, are almost always full, with 6,000 turnaways reported in 1994 in Alberta alone. We may have created more safe havens for women, but it's not over 'til it ends, and the violence hasn't ended yet.

NOTES

1. Jillian Ridington, "The Transition Process: A Feminist Environment as Reconstructive Milieu," *Victimology*, Vol. 2, No. 3/4.

2. Ibid.

WOMEN AND CHILDREN LAST

SITTING IN THE gloom of her kitchen, Eleanor wished for the moment of peace to last. There had been so few of them since she had married Bob, and even fewer since Jimmy had been born three years ago. With Bob, it was those eruptions of violence that disturbed what she had hoped would be a blissful domestic environment. And now Jimmy wouldn't stay still for a second except for this brief one. She wished for more friends too, and for more to do.

She also wished for more light, but she had resigned herself years ago to the fact that her house would not be a replica of those bright spacious sunny ones she used to admire in *Better Homes and Gardens*. Her home simply wasn't better than average, and she didn't even have a garden. She closed her eyes and transported herself to a garden where she contentedly weeded and pruned.

Suddenly, there was a piercing scream. It tore through her reverie so violently that her fist came down on the table, and half startled, half angry, she went to Jimmy. He had broken his truck. "Stop it," Eleanor warned, but Jimmy only howled. She shook him. Jimmy's eyes widened as he tried to catch his breath. He screamed louder. "It's only a truck, a toy," she fumed. How could he worry so much about a small truck giving out, when her entire life had been given up to him?

Originally published as "Child Battery," in *No Safe Place: Violence Against Women and Children*, Connie Guberman and Margie Wolfe eds. Toronto: The Women's Press, 1985.

She wrenched the truck out of his hand and walked away. But now he wanted it back, broken or not. And she gave it to him. Only she didn't give it to him, she threw it at him. It struck the boy on the side of his head, where he began to bleed, all over his clothes, on the carpet, on the towel she held against him as she tried to make it better.

◆

With the possible exception of sexual abuse, the battery of children has to be the criminal act in our society met with the most shock and anger. It seems almost inconceivable that parents could harm their children, that they would place them on hot stoves to punish them for wetting diapers, that they would bludgeon them with telephone receivers, that they would break their arms, bang their heads against walls, that these actions could be taken against children as young as four months old, and that reports of the abuse are increasing in numbers.[1] Many people are particularly confounded by the physical excesses of mothers who are not supposed to be this way, and who seem to be the living embodiment of the rejection of the female principle, the one that says that women are consistently more nurturing, more loving — naturally so — and more likely to salvage a society steeped in a grotesquely violent media and headed inexorably for nuclear annihilation.

History tells us that our own apparent dismay about child abuse is relatively new. Euthanasia was an accepted practice for unwanted children in most ancient civilizations. Children were also sold into slavery, a practice still going on in poverty stricken countries where another child can be a liability, rather than a welcome addition to a family. Not until the nineteenth century were laws created in the Western world to keep children out of the work force where they were exploited as wage-slaves and made to work in conditions that posed a danger to their safety. Elsewhere, young girls, especially, are still sold into sexual slavery or traded for goods and favours to men who can offer both. There was a time when even animals had better protection. Mary Ellis has become the classic case. She was regularly beaten by her parents in the early 1870s and was rescued in 1874 by representatives of the Society for the Prevention of Cruelty to Animals. There was no such thing as the Society for the Prevention of Cruelty to Children at the time.

The extent of society's neglect and exploitation of children can be accounted for by the fact that children had the legal status of property and property only.[2] Although in contemporary society, we tend to view children as more valuable than property or commodities, the basic status of children has not changed all that much. We still think we own our children. We still believe they reflect on our own person, rather than express any personal integrity of their own: many people have children expressly for these ego-laden reasons. Children still barely have enough credibility to have their testimony taken seriously in a court of law; the credibility of children is extremely low, especially in North America where children tend to be more sheltered than children brought up anywhere else in the world. Yet, with all of this protection, they remain remarkably vulnerable.

It is probably safe to say that the practice of child abuse does not have the same social approval per se as it may have had in the past. Still, the statistics are distressing. In the United States,[3] approximately 3 out of 100 children are kicked, bitten or punched by a parent each year. And 8 out of 100 children will experience this kind of treatment at some time before the age of 16.[4] The injuries are sometimes fatal. Why does the abuse persist? How does the syndrome begin?

Before we explore the question of how and why child battery occurs, it is crucial to examine three main elements of modern society that guarantee that the abuse will continue.

They are the sanctity of the family; the extent to which violence and authoritarianism receive constant approval within the context of a patriarchal society; and the ways in which all of us underestimate the links between soft-core abuse[5] — verbal outbursts, the odd yank of an arm, all of these expressions of parental power — and the hard-core abuse that sometimes leads to murder.

Like any other crime that takes place in the home, the statistics documenting the incidence of child abuse are likely not that accurate and represent a lower incidence than actual abuse. Child abuse takes place in private, and the privacy accorded to the family protects the perpetrators most effectively. The federal Criminal Code still exonerates child batterers from criminal liability if, according to the parent, the purpose of the battery was to discipline the child.[6] The privacy of the family — which the state violates only grudgingly when it moves in to interview — has made it almost impossible to apprehend the real violence taking place within it. Some of what we know about wife assault applies to child abuse, only the players are slightly different. Whereas men who batter are often protected by police officers who refuse to interfere in a domestic dispute because a man's home is his castle, a doctor treating a child's injuries often prefers to take the case at face value, rather than invade the sanctity of the family. Should the doctor ask, she or he would prefer to believe the parent's openly flimsy explanation rather than interfere with the parent's control over her or his child.[7]

Neighbours seldom want to interfere with the kind of parenting going on next door. For that matter, how could a neighbour, or any other concerned observer, be sure that the discipline being carried out so audibly next door is that much different or more extreme than the discipline that is part of everyday life in a family? This is a society that gives enormous reinforcement to the uses of coercion and force when disciplining children, and only within the last decade has there been any legal proscription against corporal punishment in the schools.

Barbara Pressman, in her book *Family Violence: Origins and Treatment*, makes a persuasive presentation of the extent to which we approve of violence in society and explains that parents are getting and giving double messages about it. She points to the American Commission on the Causes and Prevention of Child Abuse which cites the statistic that half the adults in America approve of teachers striking students when there is proper cause and that being noisy can be counted as one of those proper causes, according to 28 percent of the sample. If property had been damaged by the child, 67 percent of the adults would approve, and 84 percent, a startling number, would approve of corporal punishment if the child had hit someone.

What this means is that an overwhelming majority of parents agreed that it is all right for a larger, more powerful person, the school authority, to strike the child, even to show that hitting is bad. The lesson, Pressman writes, referring to what the child learns from what the parent approves, is not that hitting is inappropriate, but that physical strength and power are the appropriate means of controlling behaviour.[8]

The power hierarchy and the expression of that power by those at the top — through violence, apparently sanctioned by many adults — guarantee that child abuse will go on. Almost concurrent with the report of the American Commission on the Causes and Prevention of Child Abuse, Voice of Women, monitoring the two Canadian television networks for a 30-hour period, noted that in that time frame 249 violent conflicts were shown, totalling 1 every 7 minutes.[9] A random sampling of the products of culture — Rambo plotting revenge in Vietnam, Conan the Barbarian flexing fearsomely — shows a preoccupation with violent acts that are heroic and, according to the pornographer who brought us *Snuff* et al., erotic. The idea that violence is abhorrent in a sexist, capitalist society is wishful thinking at best. John P. Spiegel, the director of the Lemberg Center for the Study of Violence summed it up best: "Violence is not an instinct. It isn't pressure that comes from within that has to be released. It is a cultural style."[10]

We also know that many child abusers were themselves battered as children.[11] It is relatively easy to understand how victimization at an early age can lead a person to batter his or her own children: battery becomes the model for discipline and the terror that goes with it is perpetuated by a parent who thinks that developing an atmosphere of fear is the only way to get a child to do what she or he is told. It does not help that total obedience remains the standard for what defines a good child. A quiet child is assumed to be good, instead of, say, passive and acquiescent. A noisy child is considered bad instead of, say, active and curious. For the most part, parents receive no alternative to punitive and authoritarian practices to keep the bad kids in line. Many of the batterers who were themselves the recipients of harsh disciplinary punishment believe somehow that the experience was good for them.

We live in a society that has conceived and carried out full-scale wars, perhaps the plainest evidence of our collective acceptance of violent solutions to the problem of conflict. And we are growing less, not more, sensitive to how violence really feels. Recent data indicates that prolonged exposure to explicit violence (and explicit sexual violence, though this is not relevant here) desensitizes viewers to the harm caused by the violence.[12] We ought to wonder what the connection is between that tendency and the one Mary Van Stolk describes when she talks about how parents who batter tend to underestimate the extent of the force they are using.[13]

This last fact, the trend toward underestimating how much force we use, is relevant to all of us who have either had children or had any contact with them. Before we smugly disdain child abusers for their absence of control, we should take into account our own experiences. Anyone who has had to sit with a youngster for more than an afternoon may herself comprehend how quickly the breaking point approaches. How many times have we hollered at a child without having any idea how terrifying the experience may be for that child? How many of us have yanked a kid's arm to stop that child from picking up an object she or he may have dropped? Why do we think that this kind of controlling behaviour is significantly different from the actions of the child abuser? Because we do it for the child's good? That is precisely what many child batterers argue. Many researchers have devised a spectrum of child abuse that begins with verbal and emotional outbursts — the kind many of us have all the time — and escalates to hard-core battery and sometimes murder. In a way, we are all complicit in the hard-core abuse as long as we shrug off our own soft-core excesses.

Given our definitions of what a good child is, given the reinforcement of harsh disciplinary measures, given the inundation of media endorsing violent behaviour, given the extent to which most of us have become desensitized to violence just by seeing the nightly news, given the fast-blurring line between soft- and hard-core abuse, which fades precisely because we are all desensitized in this culture, it is a wonder that the incidence of child abuse is as infrequent as it is. From a feminist perspective, the numerous conditions under which anyone can scream at a child, shake a child, pull him, push her, precisely because we are in positions of power in relation to children, should be recognized, if not as abusive, then at least as too close to abusive for comfort.

To appreciate how close we come to being abusive to our children merely in the course of our daily parenting is to begin a process of understanding how child abuse works. The line between soft-core abuse — yelling, dominating, using our children as extensions of our own egos — and the hard-core violence that maims and injures is a very slender one. What is crucial is that each of us as parents has the power to damage our kids, whether we use that power or not. Thus, the carte blanche of parents has to be questioned and challenged. Moreover, as we will discover, the fact that some parents do graduate from soft-core power-plays to hard-core violence is explained by social forces.

Still, it is the most vicious type of child-beating that is the subject here, the kind that inflicts physical injury on the child. It used to be that this kind of child battery was assumed to be committed mostly by women, but newer data suggests that women do not necessarily beat their children more than men do. At this point, we should be prepared to say that women and men beat their children in equal numbers.[14] But the similarities end there. In a sexist society, men batter their children because they have power. Women batter their children because they have little power, except the power they can exercise over their children.

The adage 'a man's home is his castle' is still relevant in most North American families. Regardless of what traditionalists and some segments of the child-protection movement say, a man who batters his children is not evidence of a family falling apart, he is evidence that the family remains the locus of male power which stays protected and intact. Child abuse occurs in families whose hierarchies are only marginally more extreme than that of the average family.[15] Men are on top and children are on the bottom, as evidenced by the actions of an abusive father.

The particular conditions in which the father might find himself are relevant only to a point. It is true that financial stress, for example, is sometimes a factor contributing to child abuse.[16] But this kind of stress does not get acted out on a child in a total vacuum. Power is the key. If the family structure did not give the father the power to batter his children and, crucially, to get away with it, he would not beat them, regardless of the state of his finances.[17] The missing link between financial stress and child abuse is self-esteem.

Financial problems and their blow to the ego conflict strongly with that power afforded to fathers and to their self-perception as the embodiment of parental authority. And, when a father's self-esteem is damaged, he will be more inclined to exercise his authority, to let everyone know who is running the show.[18] How many times have you heard of situations in which mothers, unable to say no, direct children to their fathers who have no difficulty laying down the law? Mom is soft, Dad is tough as nails, a disciplinarian who believes he is not fulfilling his role as a parent unless he throws his weight around.

It is not as if he gets no reinforcement for what he is doing. He is just being a regular fellow, trying to adjust to what is expected. Read a portrait of the typical child abuser: hard-hearted, no nurturing sense, inarticulate and unable to express feelings, controlling, intimidating, able to back up his demands with the threat of physical force.[19] It sounds more like James Bond than anyone else. And, while it is true that the male abuser, who is often unemployed[20] and a substance abuser,[21] does not exactly have the ideal curriculum vitae, his personality is the model for our cultural standards of masculinity.

Researchers looking at the child-abuse syndrome avoid this kind of analysis assiduously, or so it seems. They insist that something is going terribly wrong when a father abuses a child,[22] not that the universe is unfolding in the way that patriarchal norms are established. We live in a society where men have power in the family. We live in a society where violence is a cultural style. We also live in a society where violence is a cultural style belonging especially to men. Very little work has been done to make the connections between society's expectations of men: that they be predisposed to a machismo celebrated relentlessly in everything from organized sports — where assault is encouraged, made entertaining and sometimes part of the rules of the game — to pornography where violence is eroticized and fused with male sexuality, to violence in the home. In turn, male violence reinforces for children all the rigid sex roles that contributed to the violence in the first place.

The attitude that men have an inherent right to power and its expression is already well on its way to development when young boys know enough to separate themselves from trivial girlish pastimes; when Rambo becomes a role model; when men learn that wives are supposed to cater to their needs; and when they open their eyes wide enough to see the products of a $7-billion-dollar pornography industry[23] that lets them buy access to female sexuality. The ways in which male power can be exercised are intensely promoted by the media, so that it is unlikely that men will know an alternative to power-tripping and a preoccupation with violence. They may never know what nurturing feels like. This means that especially well-socialized men are bound to be disasters around children.

Children, by their nature, grate on the nerves of strict disciplinarians, who are accustomed to getting their way and to maintaining control over situations. A child's spontaneity will aggravate a man who does not want any interruptions in his neatly ordered life. A child's curiosity will annoy a man who believes he knows everything and who therefore has no patience with someone, even a child, who does not. A child who is loud is bad news for a man who likes to choose who will make noise and when. A child's playfulness is trivial to a father who takes everything seriously, especially his own power. Children are demanding, they have needs — something men are taught to monopolize. Sometimes children distract mothers from meeting fathers' needs. In short, children get in the way. A father's pre-violent resistance to a child almost guarantees that the child's demands will grow louder and that the situation will escalate to become violent. Although all of this sometimes applies to the female child abuser, it is not, as we will see later, the main dynamic at work in the case of female child batterers.

We can learn a great deal about fathers battering children

from what we know about wife assault. The same power men have over women, and the fact that they batter because they are permitted to do so, applies to fathers and children as well. Sometimes the connection between child assault and wife assault is painfully close. In 20 percent of the situations in which men are beating their children, they are beating their wives as well.[24] Battery of children often begins at pregnancy when one outburst can damage two victims.[25]

The anger men feel toward their pregnant wives and their children-to-be is often related to their inability to cope financially with an addition to the family. As we will see further on, access to the freedom to choose pregnancy would probably make for fewer abused children, but it is not clear that a potentially abusive father would agree to the termination of a pregnancy if his assent reflected his own inability to support a family. There are many factors to be weighed here. As long as men are the head of families and wield power in the traditional family's unequal context, they will not likely concede personal failure and agree to their wives having abortions. Instead, the wives will have children and the husbands will continue to believe that they have a right to beat all the family members, and that this is, in fact, expected of them and that their world will fall apart if they do not.

Researchers, both those who accept the psychopathological model and those who understand that social factors are important, will accept many explanations for why men beat their children — except for the obvious one that men have power, especially in the family and need to have it reinforced even if the ones they are supposed to be caring for are hurt by it. Similarly, the literature on female battery rings false to the feminist ear. Sometimes the researchers, Ray Helfer and C. Kempe among them, will be relatively generous and attribute the battery to the mother's battery as a child. But, most of the time, the literature, especially that espousing the psychodynamic and psychopathological approaches to child abuse, reeks of assumptions of what is natural among women.[26]

Seldom does the research address the social context that sets women up for profound disappointment in their lives as mothers. The result is an unsympathetic view of the female child batterer as monster, not only because she beats her children, but because, in so doing, she subverts mother nature.[27] This is an especially biased view compared with the view of the male child batterer who is working out the experience of his battery as a child, often at the hands of yet another unnatural woman, his mother. In seeking a more sympathetic approach to child battery in the hands of women, I am not suggesting that women do not hurt their children when they beat them, or that the abuse should be excused. What is at issue here is the tendency among researchers to bring their own sexist values to the investigation, so that men are excused (read: it was their mother's faults) and women are villified (read: they are sick and unnatural).[28]

What gets left out is this: for adult men, adult life at the top of the family hierarchy is the payoff; to abuse is their right. For women, adult life at the bottom is a trauma; to abuse is relief, even if the feeling is only temporary and overwhelmed by consuming guilt.

Brandt Steele, a psychologist, attributes female battery of children to the breakdown of the mother's ability to mother a child. He refers, throughout his work, to the distortion of her deep, sensitive, intuitive awareness and response to the infant's conditions and needs, and to her desire that her children satisfy her needs.[29] Why does he call these expectations unreasonable? Why is he so surprised that women expect that children will do something for them and that is what children are there for? Society, until recently rocked by the demands and insights of the women's movement, insisted that child-rearing was the only way a woman could fulfill herself in life. Why should we be so surprised that women want to get something out of it?

Child abusers come from all backgrounds.[30] Regardless of class, female abusers share a feeling of being imprisoned by their role as mothers.[31] This is a role women are encouraged to enjoy lest they lose economic support from a man and lose status as human beings. One family planning counsellor described how pregnant teenagers believe that the only way they can achieve status or value as human beings was by becoming a mother.[32] A lot of work is done to convince women that they are supposed to like the role and that childbirth is the ultimate achievement. It starts when little girls play with dolls and the socialization continues relentlessly as magazines for homemakers pour on the positive reinforcement for the creative acts of housekeeping and child-rearing.

What the researchers who examine the breakdown of mothering fail to note is that many women are in the home via the coercion of social conditioning and that, if this conditioning were not so effective, many women who have no desire to care for children would not be in positions to have them. In other words, sexism's excessive — and false — advertising for the value of the nuclear family and the relative roles within it has a great deal to do with creating the battered-child syndrome.

'No,' say the exponents of defective socialization, whose ideas harken back to the question, Why can't she just be a good mother like everybody else? This trivializes women's real experience in the world. Feminists might argue the opposite, that child abusers have been socialized too well. Entirely prepared for a blissful life in which motherhood will empower them, many women are led into situations where there is little satisfaction, and even less power. This means that, like well-socialized men, well-socialized women will be disasters around children. Children will become the scapegoats, the only ones with less power than the angry women who are supposed to care for them.

Having been prepared for heaven on earth in the home,

the well-conditioned woman proceeds with her life as pre-
scribed only to discover that babies do not give unconditional
love, they cry a lot instead. They do not obey on command
because they appreciate what their mothers have done for
them; they just demand more and more. They do not wet
their diapers at convenient times or bellow for food on cue.
There is little financial reward for the job and even less mobility. For women who have been told only the upside of the
housewife's story, the real experience of motherhood makes
for an alienation that is profound. And there is no escape,
either for the mother or the child. To leave the baby alone is
to neglect it, and to be guilty of what is called soft(er) abuse.
To stay is to make the child vulnerable to a rage that, in spite
of how it is vented, comes from somewhere legitimate.

Still, Steele, and other exponents of psychodynamism,
wonder how it is that child abusers do not affect the child-
mother bond so important to child-rearing. Mary Van Stolk
wisely questions the practice of wrenching children away
from their mothers at birth to be put in the more expert care
of medical doctors, thus pointing out the contradiction
between society's expectations of mothers and the actions of
society's institutions.[33]

But few observers have ever suggested that the child-
mother bond may not exist because of the woman's experience during pregnancy, or because that woman may never
have wanted the child in the first place. It may be that the
abuse of the child begins in pregnancy when women con-
sume alcohol or drugs that put the fetus at risk. What addicts
women to alcohol? we should be asking. What makes them
have to avoid reality? What about the child battery that
begins when a husband beats his spouse? What we know
about battering husbands is that their assault grows more
vicious when the victim is pregnant.[34] She is held responsible
for the child; her pregnancy is her failure and bodes for the
imminent failure of the father to provide for his family.

Consider then, if a woman's pregnancy provokes a violent attack from her husband, what attitudes she may develop toward the child? Is it not possible that she could blame the child for the assault? Or lash out at it?

Is this a wanted child? Rarely, except in feminist literature, has the fact that women do not control their reproductive choices ever been linked to the incidence of child abuse. While it is true that many battering parents want their children, they want them to be other than the way they are. Many battering parents never wanted their babies and considered them burdens from the beginning.[35] When a couple is unable to afford a child, they should have the choice as to whether or not they should have the child. If a woman in a battery situation leaves herself more vulnerable to a brutal attack, she should have the option of terminating her pregnancy. Many will argue that abortion is the ultimate in child abuse. But this romanticization of the fetus makes it impossible to mitigate the misery battered women often experience in pregnancy and consigns an unwanted child to what could be a childhood in hell.

And what about a woman's hellish life within the family? Freedom to choose pregnancy does not entail only choosing when to cope with having a child and terminating the pregnancy when times demand it. Reproductive freedom is real when pregnant women have the self-determination to walk out the door of a battery situation and have the resources to keep their children and rear them. But these circumstances do not occur frequently, and women, whether battered or just controlled, find themselves locked into situations which they do not feel they can change.

A study by Murray Straus in 1979 surveyed families with children between the ages of one and a half and five years and puts the matter into perspective. Straus discovered that what really caused women to lose control was closely associated with the female sex roles.[36] So now consider a typical portrait of the conditions of a female child abuser: responsibility for toilet-training, for training children to eat and to sleep on command (infants tend to be recalcitrant on all three counts), too much housework, marital disharmony, isolation in the house, financial worries. This could be almost any woman. Most of these conditions are going to be factors in the lives of housewives unless child rearing and housework are shared in the home. As for financial worries, these are epidemic among women, who make sixty cents on the male dollar;[37] who work part time when they would rather have full-time employment;[38] who, if they are sole-support mothers, can expect social assistance programs that still leave them short of the poverty line since their benefits are only 63 percent to this line.[39]

The point here is this: the conditions of men and women within a patriarchal society set both sexes up so that abuse of their children is actually quite likely. Men, socialized to hide their feelings of love and encouraged to express their dominance, take seriously their roles as authoritarians in the family. The fact that violence is the culturally acceptable way for men to express their power leads to the child-abuse syndrome. Women, on the other hand, discover the false promise of life within the nuclear family and, out of frustration, lash out in socially sanctioned ways — physical punishment — at the only ones more vulnerable than themselves. The family institutionalizes it all, for as the family is the locus of male power, it is also the locus of female powerlessness.

More crucially, this could happen to anyone. The tendency among observers of child abusers is to identify them as anomalies — people out there, not people like ourselves. But we are all socialized intensely to conform to male and female sex roles. We are all part of the social order's cultural style of violence, especially when it comes to our children. None of this would persist as it does unless children remained as devalued as they are. Physically attacking them, subjecting them to emotional abuse, allowing our frustration to come out at them, keeps children in their place as likely targets. If you are a woman who has heard her child whine too much and has let go with a torrent of verbal abuse — even just yelling, "shut up," at the top of your lungs — then you know what I am talking about.

♦

As consciousness of the existence of the child-abuse syndrome has increased, professionals who have contact with children have been encouraged to improve their process of identifying abuse. Under the auspices of various provincial child-abuse programs, handbooks have been developed for physicians to assist in the first phase of combatting child abuse — the detection phase. Through these handbooks, medical doctors have been encouraged to recognize the symptoms and to take a more pro-active role in dealing with patients and with their parents. Many doctors have resisted, in keeping with the Western medical model which addresses the injury itself and not the conditions that precipitated it. But their associations have supported the new initiatives. Teachers too have taken a stronger stand. In light of new policies generated within their federations, they face the risk of losing their jobs if they fail to report suspected instances of child abuse.

In the meantime, in the post-detection phase, the Children's Aid Societies have remained entrenched in their process of trying to maintain the nuclear family at all costs. Certainly the CAS has become more aware of and has taken action on the need for better housing and for community day care that is accessible, but still, CAS principles have centred around preserving the family, the institution whose protection often perpetuates the conditions that engender child abuse in the first place. The issue is not only that the CAS parachutes into homes, removing children, bringing them back, removing them again in a dizzying yo-yo effect, but also that actions of CAS workers affect men and women differently.

This should not come as a surprise since an abusive mother's relationship to her child is different from an abusive father's. Children are often in the way of their abusive fathers, while children are often the very essence of the identity of their abusive mothers. Women who beat their children do love them and lose something precious when a child is being taken away from them. An abusive mother has a great deal at stake in her children, possibly too much, which is often the very difficulty that she acts out through violence. When a woman subsumes her identity in her children, when she attacks them because their naughtiness reflects badly on her, when she can have no identity without her children, she crumbles when they are no longer there.

If the mother is the abuser and the CAS worker removes the child, the separation from the mother is traumatic and usually reinforces her lack of self-esteem. If she is in a battery situation with her husband, the consequences can be especially damaging when the actions of the state seem to sanction his abuse of her. If she cannot take care of the child, to the extent that the CAS has to race in to the rescue, then the husband's abuse of the mother receives justification.

Jeffrey Wilson, a family lawyer and one of Canada's most eloquent and effective advocates of children's rights, agrees that maybe the movement has gone too far, that no one is considering the needs of parents, that the courts are entirely unsympathetic to the experience of women who are at the bottom of a rigid hierarchy that makes it impossible for them to recover their children once they have been forced to give them up.[40] At least abusive fathers, if they want to see their children, have more resources to hire legal counsel and, regardless, do not share the feeling that without children they have no identity.

We have to be very careful as we argue that social structures and patriarchal institutions operate to condemn men and women equally to becoming abusive parents; only one half of the argument, the half about women, is likely to get heard. Women have less clout in the legal system and less credibility with government agencies in a sexist society. We may be very clear about how male sex roles automatically cast men as child abusers, but the more we say that the conditions of women — the way we are defined targeted for abuse, denied freedom of choice over who we can be and over our reproduction, denied economic parity with men — forecasts the battery of children, the more we have to guard against the agents of the state and those of other repositories of power identifying all women as unfit mothers and acting accordingly. Kathleen Lahey put it this way:

> I suspect that even if [the] point is that vast institutional changes have to be made if life is to be safe for women and thus for children [this approach] will be taken as simply saying that women are not fit mothers. And that is only a short step from saying that male members of the state, who are the policy makers anyway, are better able to decide how children are to be raised and by whom. The whole concept of fitness for motherhood plays directly into the hands of judges and legislators who would thus be able to resolve the patriarchal impulse toward control over women and reproduction.[41]

In December 1983, the Standing Committee on Social Development submitted its report on child abuse to the Ontario Legislature. The report focussed solely on legislative approaches to the problem, and the legislative options consistently dealt with the safety of the child. There was virtually no mention of root causes of child battery, no analysis of the social forces that perpetuate it, and only a passing, seemingly pop-psychological reference to the absence of touch in the child-rearing practices of the abusers or to the batterers' unrealistic expectations of their children.

This is the kind of report we usually toss aside as either superficial or too legislation-oriented to be of much use, except that the report did make one small suggestion about which preventative measures might be considered in the future. Kathleen Lahey's fears of state excesses might be all too well founded. The report referred to testimonies of witnesses who stressed the need for an effective screening system during prenatal and postnatal periods to help detect cases that pose a high risk of child abuse.

In some hospitals in England every pregnant woman who is admitted to give birth is assigned a nurse or social worker who counsels and determines whether she is a high-risk individual. If a high- or moderate-risk situation is detected, contact is maintained with the family for six months.[42]

What is a high-risk case? One public health official testified that the failure of the mother to touch or cuddle her baby ought to be a crucial indicator.[43] Then what? and says whom? Remove the child? On what basis? This notion of pre-screening is as close as the report comes to discussing ways of preventing abuse (the rest prevents re-abuse) and evokes the spectre of the state and its mechanisms swooping in to decide who and how children should be reared, exchanging the hardship of the child for the hardship of the parent. Feminists must begin to make some crucial distinctions. We have to accept that the privacy in the home and the family is not sacred and support a physician or teacher who identifies a case of child abuse and does something about it. At the same time, we have to establish that pre-screening is state intervention in the extreme, approximates a new eugenics, and approaches totalitarianism.

The government's approach has been consistent in recognizing that the safety of the child comes first, and this is a priority with which it is too difficult to argue. But patriarchal institutions, and by that I mean government agencies and hospitals and the medical establishment generally, seem to be unable to deal with this priority without appropriating all reproductive functions as well as women's lives in general. It is not only pre-screening for child abuse that has to be examined here, but that recommendation, whether accepted or not, combined with paternalistic abortion laws, proscriptions against midwifery, and persecution of anyone who wants to give birth other than in a hospital. Power is power no matter where it is applied, and feminists have to be vigilant, questioning at all times the state's motives and increasing clout in the area of reproductive choice.

The feminist agenda also has to include the provision of an integrated strategy for dealing with and understanding child abuse. The strategy must centre on the roots of women's oppression and the essential oppression of sex roles so as to make comprehensible the battery of children at the hands of their parents. First, we have to understand that beating up children is consistent with what is expected of fathers who conform to sex-role stereotypes, and we have to use that consciousness to alter our expectations of what men should be. Care for children, real care for children, must cease being divorced from traditional male activity. Right from the time they are boys and sneer at the idea of playing with dolls, men have resisted caring for children.

Second, the glorification of the nuclear family has got to stop. Too many women are lied to about what family life will be like for them and, because they believe this is their only choice, they blame themselves for their grief and frustration and cannot imagine changing their lives. Indeed, the nuclear family has to be exposed for what it is — a dangerous place for women and children.

Traditionally the privacy of the family has been sacrosanct. Now we know that keeping family matters private has protected the perpetrators of violence within it. As long as the family remains hierarchical, with fathers on the top, they can exercise their authority through brutality, and mothers try to gain authority in the same way. As long as total authority is vested in parents, children will be vulnerable to attack and neighbours will mind their own business while the discipline is being meted out; family members will be discouraged from talking about it; the exclusivity of the family will continue to isolate its members, especially mothers, from contact with other people or from activities nor related to child-rearing.

The entire structure of child-rearing has to change. Every child should be a wanted child. This is not to say that mothers who beat their children do not love them, but rather, that a child who is born by choice is less likely to be kicked in utero by the father and even less likely to be viewed as an enemy, as Mary Van Stolk describes the feeling,[44] once it has been brought into the world. If every woman had the freedom to choose, the incidence of child abuse would go down; if better and affordable day care were available so that women were more mobile in their everyday lives, then the conditions referred to by researchers as stress and frustrations would surely abate.

If financial stress is among these conditions, then the reallocation of resources is also in order. This redistribution of wealth is relevant, not only to reduce the disparity between poor, middle-income, and wealthy families, but to reduce the disparity between men and women as well. Women must be paid equally for work of equal value; the benefits to sole-support mothers have to increase. Most important, the means of making mothering and child-rearing — women's work — valued in our society must be developed. Would a father taking care of children not feel less disgusted with the job if he did not have contempt for what women do? And what is a fit mother in our society but one who chooses to consign herself to hundreds of hours of work a week with no pay and with few immediate rewards?

Finally, we must come to grips with the fact that the celebration of violence is our cultural style; that capitalism and sexism depend on the maintenance of power over others — over women and children in particular; that power and who has it is related to the incidence of child abuse; that men and women know few other ways to exercise that power without using force and intimidation over their own children and, in the case of husbands, over their wives as well. A redistribution of wealth is crucial, but so is a redistribution of power. As it stands, children do not have a chance. We need to take them more seriously, and we need to recognize our own complicity in the child-abuse syndrome. Each of us has been impatient with a child; we've wished for blessed relief from their constant demands; we consider vacations an escape from them; we've yelled, pulled, and yanked at them, when they have not the slightest opportunity of fighting back and achieving self-determination. We use their dependence on us as a means of justifying our power over them. All of this devalues them.

If children had more power, they would be less vulnerable. They would not be made scapegoats for violence at the hands of women who, as it is, can lash out at no one else. If women had more power, if they had more life choices, they would not be shunted into the home where isolation and disappointment foster the frustration that triggers a violent attack on their children. If men had less power, if fathers were not expected to mete out physical punishment in the name of authority, if violent and aggressive behaviour were not so quintessentially male in the patriarchal scheme of things, so many children would not be terrorized by parental abuse. In short, change the power dynamics in society, and there will be fewer beaten children.

UPDATE 1995

Experts in the area say that it continues to be difficult to obtain reliable statistics on child abuse. So much of what constitutes abuse continues to be legal if it takes place at the hands of caretakers, that reporting is consistently low. Yet, the

Kids' Help Phone Line, which receives phone calls from children in distress from around the country, reports that of the close to 1,000 calls the service receives a day, approximately 10 percent are related to problems stemming from child abuse or child sexual abuse.

Still, awareness among professionals has developed to a certain extent. In Canada, teachers' unions have attempted to educate their members and, in some jurisdictions, teachers are obligated to report on child abuse if they believe it is happening in a student's home. Doctors, too, have become sensitized to the fact that children coming into emergency rooms for treatment of repeat accidents may be at risk.

But the courts in Canada continue to interpret section 43 of Canada's criminal code in a way that legalizes behaviours that are plainly abusive.

Section 43 states that "a caretaker, whether teacher, parent or parental stand-in can be justified in using force against a child by way of correction ... if the force does not exceed what is reasonable." Last year, US tourist Richard Pearson got angry at his five-year-old daughter for closing the car door on her younger brother's hand. The Pearson's car was parked in a public lot in London, Ontario — there were people around. Pearson took his daughter, hit her four times, threw her over the trunk of the car, yanked down her pants and hit her again eight times. The intensity of her screams moved a passerby to call the police.

It has been reported that the passerby told Pearson that what he was doing was illegal in Canada — it's good to know an average Canadian understands children's rights. But the courts did not agree and acquitted him. What became interesting about the case is the extent of public support Pearson received. His case, in fact, became a flashpoint for the outpouring of public opinion that parents can do whatever they feel like to discipline their kids, providing hard evidence that children remain the most vulnerable in our population.

NOTES

1. In her article "The Battered Baby Syndrome," in Mary Alice Beyer Gammon, ed., *Violence in Canada,* (Toronto: Methuen, 1978), Gammon describes reports as having increased in Ontario by 52.5 percent between the years 1972 and 1976 (p. 94).

2. Kathleen Lahey, "Research on Child Abuse in a Liberal Patriarchy," in Jill McCalla Vickers, ed., *Taking Sex into Account* (Ottawa: Carlton University Press, 1984), pp. 160-161.

3. Unfortunately, the American data overwhelms Canadian statistics. We do have some, based on reports of various Children Aids Societies, but Canadian researchers, among them Mary Van Stolk, author of *The Battered Child in Canada* (Toronto: McClelland and Stewart, 1978), p. 3, agree that an accurate statistical picture is difficult to obtain. Further references to Van Stolk appear in the text.

4. Richard Gelles, "A Profile of Violence toward Children in the U.S." in George Gerbner, Catherine Ross, and Edward Zigler, eds., *Child Abuse: An Agenda for Action* (New York: Oxford University. Press, 1980), p. 87. Further references to this work appear in the text.

5. 'Hard core' and 'soft core' are terms coined in Mary Van Stolk's book. I have used them here knowing they evoke the issue of pornography, pornography being the arena in which these terms are normally used. They help to make the connection between violence in the home and our pornographic culture.

6. Section 43 of the Criminal Code reads: "Every school teacher, parent or person standing in the place of the parent is justified in using force by way of correction towards a pupil or child as the case may be, who is under his care, if the force does not exceed what is reasonable

under the circumstances." Note the use of the legal language 'correction' and not, say, protection from danger.

7. Mary Van Stolk, *The Battered Child in Canada*, p. 38.

8. Barbara Pressman, *Family Violence: Origin and Treatments* (Guelph, Ont.: Children's Aid Society and Family Counselling Services/University of Guelph, 1984), pp. 96-97. Pressman quotes Lewis Harris's poll taken in 1968.

9. These statistics are taken from an unpublished paper by L. Swift, prepared by the Edmonton Branch of Voice of Women in 1969. For an extensive and very useful discussion of violence and television and its effects on children, see George Gerbner's "Children and Power on Television," in *Child Abuse: An Agenda for Action*.

10. J.H. Pollack, "An Interview with Dr. John D. Spiegel: What You Can Do to Help Stop Violence," *Family Circle* (Oct. 1968), p. 79.

11. There are many who have discovered this, especially Ray Helfer and C. Henry Kempe. Helfer edited the book *The Battered Child* (Chicago: University of Chicago Press, 1980), which is something of a primer and is now in its third edition. But another good source comes from M.J. Paulson and P. R. Blake, "The Abused, Battered and Maltreated Child: A Review," *Trauma* 9, No. 4 (Dec. 1967), pp. 56-57.

12. Dr. Ed Donnerstein's work on explicit violence and pornography is crucial in this area. In testimony given at hearings on pornography in Minneapolis, Donnerstein summarized his research, saying, "Subjects who have seen violent material or x-rated material see less injury to a rape victim than people who have not seen these films." Public Hearings on Ordinances to Add Pornography as Discrimnation against Women, Committee on Government Operations, City Council, Minneapolis, Minn., 12-13 Dec. 1983. Transcript, 1, 37-38 (unpublished).

13. Van Stolk, *The Battered Child In Canada*, p. 115.

14. Ibid., p. 6.

15. Clearly, the more inequality in the home, the greater the risk of severe parental violence. Gelles, "A Profile of Violence." p. 102.

16. Ibid., p. 97.

17. Gelles makes a point of saying that "... it would be a mistake to infer that poverty is the sole cause of violence" Gelles "A Profile of Violence," p. 97.

18. Gammon's article "The Battered Baby Syndrome" traces and charts an interactional model of child abuse developed through the work of S. Wasserman, David Gil, and Richard Gelles, which incorporates frustration and self-esteem as factors in child abuse (pp. 104-105).

19. This is a composite portrait of mine based on a number of readings. "Hardhearted" refers to Van Stolk's claim that parents do not feel anything when they beat their children (Van Stolk, *The Battered Child in Canada*, p. 16); no nurturing sense refers to the inability to create the parent — child bond, a feature of Brands Steele's "Psychodynamic Factors in Child Abuse", in *The Battered Child*, pp. 49-85; controlling and intimidating refers to the tendency already mentioned of child abusers to be harsh disciplinarians who need to express their own authority. Finally, I think that men's greater size and the extent to which they are taught as young boys to use their bodies, afford them the ability to back up their demands with physical force.

20. Gelles, "A Profile of Violence ...," p. 97.

21. Van Stolk, *The Battered Child in Canada*, p. 9.

22. See the work of Brandt Steele and J.H. Pollack, in particular their "A Psychiatric Study of Parents Who Abuse Infants and Small Children," in *The Battered Child*. The

work of Serapio Zalba, such as "Treatment of Child Abuse," in Suzanne K. Steinmetz and Murray A. Straus, eds., *Violence in the Family* (New York: Dodd Mead, 1975), is also key in this area.

23. See "The Place of Pornography," *Harper's* (Nov. 1984), p. 31.

24. Testimony of Douglas J. Besharov, Director, National Center on Child Abuse and Neglect, before the House of Representatives Committee on Science and Technology, 14 Feb. 1978. Transcript, pp. 17-18.

25. Van Stolk, *The Battered Child in Canada*, p. 6.

26. This is essentially the substance of the psychopathological model for child abuse as expressed by Zalba and others. This was the first clinical approach to child abuse and crucially centres on a blame-the-victim model, and was done at a time when women were assumed to be major perpetrators of violence against children.

27. Edward Zigler, author of "Controlling Child Abuse: Do We Have the Knowledge and/or the Will?," in *Child Abuse*, agrees: "The notion that child abusers lack maternal instinct has reinforced the anger and revulsion associated with child abuse"(p. 4). Indeed, the book *Child Abuse* is a collection of essays designed to further a social, rather than an individual, approach.

28. Kathleen Lahey's "Research on Child Abuse in a Liberal Patriarchy," in *Taking Sex into Account*, synthesizes the research and describes its biases.

29. Steele, "Psychodynamic Factors in Child Abuse," in *The Battered Child*, pp. 49-85.

30. Van Stolk, *The Battered Child in Canada*, p. 7.

31. Murray Straus, "Family Patterns and Child Abuse in a Nationally Representative American Sample," *Child Abuse and Neglect*, 3 (1979), pp. 213-225.

32. Susan G. Cole, Interview with Elizabeth Parker, Director, Family Planning Services, Toronto, 4 June 1981.

33. Van Stolk, *The Battered Child in Canada,* p. 45.

34. This is based on my interviews with assaulted women when I prepared "Home Sweet Home?," an article I wrote for Maureen Fitzgerald, Connie Guberman, and Margie Wolfe, eds., *Still Ain't Satisfied! Canadian Feminism Today* (Toronto: Women's Press, 1982), pp. 55-67.

35. This is Mary Van Stolk's explanation for the abuse of the fetus in vitro via alcohol and drug abuse (p. 45).

36. Straus, "Family Patterns and Child Abuse," pp. 213-225.

37. Most recent data from Statistics Canada.

38. According to the most recent data from Statistics Canada, 72 percent of women work part time and over half of those would prefer a full-time job.

39. The New Democratic Caucus, *The Other Ontario: A Report on Poverty in Ontario* (Toronto: New Democratic Caucus, June 1984), p. 17.

40. Susan G. Cole, Interview with Jeffrey Wilson, Toronto, 7 Oct. 1984.

41. Lahey, "Research in Child Abuse," p. 116.

42. Standing Committee on Social Development, *Second Report on Family Violence: Child Abuse* (Toronto: Government of Ontario, Dec. 1983), p. 11.

43. Ibid.

44. "The mother and the child are in conflict and the lines of battle are drawn." (Van Stolk, *The Battered Child in Canada* , p. 20.)

FURTHER READING

BOOKS

Elizabeth Camden. *If He Comes Back He's Mine.* Toronto: Women's Press, 1984.

George Gerbner, Catherine J. Ross, and Edward Zigler, eds. *Child Abuse. An Agenda for Action.* New York: Oxford University Press, 1980.

Barbara Pressman. *Family Violence: Origins and Treatments.* Guelph, Ont.: The City of Guelph, Children's Aid Society and Family Counselling Services/University of Guelph, 1984.

Mary Van Stolk. *The Battered Child in Canada.* Toronto: McClelland and Stewart, 1978.

ARTICLES

Mary Alice Beyer Gammon. "The Battered Baby Syndrome: A Reconceptualization of Family Conflict." In Mary Alice Beyer Gammon, ed., *Violence in Canada.* Toronto: Methuen, 1978, pp. 93-111.

Kathleen Lahey. "Research on Child Abuse in a Liberal Patriarchy." In Jill Vickers, ed., *Taking Sex into Account.* Ottawa: Carlton University Press, 1984, pp. 56-84.

Murray Straus. "Family Patterns — Child Abuse in a Nationally Representative American Sample." *Child Abuse and Neglect* 3 (1979), pp. 213-225.

SEXUALIZING VIOLENCE

TAKEN AT FACE value, the term *radical feminism* is redundant. Why is it necessary to apply the adjective *radical* to a body of ideas and a political project that takes on all the dimensions of social life and looks to reweave entirely our social fabric? But as the new wave of feminism took off in the seventies, with groups choosing specific emphases for their work and analysis, the era of the compound feminist began. We had socialist-feminists, liberal-feminists, lesbian-feminists, later eco-feminists, pro-sex-feminists and a movement juggling new priorities and awarenesses of the social dynamics of class, race, discrimination on the basis of age, disability and more. So diverse were these groupings that French feminists went so far as to say that feminism did not exist anymore. It was more accurate to call them feminisms.

And so one of those feminisms became known as radical feminism. It was the issue of violence against women that gave radical feminism its spark, and what distinguished radical feminism from its sister groups. By naming what was happening to women, by using terms that had not made their way into public consciousness, let alone public policy, radical feminists tugged away at public awareness until the unspoken came out of its closet. We talked about rape, violence against women in the home, sexual harassment and more recently about incest. As activists and sociologists tried to make sense

Parts of this article originally appeared as "The Sex Factor in Violence," *Broadside*, August/September 1989.

of the crisis, feminist research, the kind that listened to women, uncovered the truth that sexual abuse was epidemic, not occasional, more normal than marginal.

The violence issues became the bedrock of radical feminism in part because they gave feminists the inspiration to develop a particular method and process. Speakouts, in which women shared their experiences, became an important part of ending the isolation experienced by abuse survivors and of helping to identify the specificity of women's experience of male domination. The abuse crossed class, race and ethnic lines in a way that charged a radical analysis of women's oppression. We might have different coloured skins, cultural backgrounds, class and able-ist privileges, all of which influenced where and how we experienced the abuse and whether and how fast we could heal, but the fact of violence remained a constant fact of life.

The discussions never remained wholly abstract. There was real experience, pain and trauma to confront. In shelters and rape crisis centres, radical feminist activists and counsellors guided survivors through what was usually a hostile legal system and helped them get on with their lives. It is a little known fact that Toronto's Interval House was the world's first women's shelter to open its doors to assaulted women. These centres took on what seemed like the overwhelming task of educating the public and smashing the ancient and very resilient myths about violence against women.

While the mainstream media boast of bringing it all out into the open, we know that everything we learned about sexual abuse arose out of someone's pain and our then radical notion that women ought to be believed when they spoke about their experience. Being politically active, respecting women and women-centered perspectives became a more important criteria for workers in shelters and in sexual assault centres than any professional degree tacked onto the end of a counsellor's name.

We defined the terms, whether inside or outside feminism. We built shelters. We put the issues on the public agenda. Now we have to keep moving and thinking.

I think that the original analyses we forged about the violence issues may have missed some important ambiguities and complexities. Those analyses were important, radical usually, but sometimes only half right and in one or two cases, if not wrong, then at least a bit too simplistic. New information is forcing us to reject some of our more rigid formulations. Accepting the fact that the violence issues need some re-examination is, in my view, central to feminism's future.

The key to our original thinking was the principle that violence against women in its various forms is about power and not about sex. I no longer believe this tidy formulation. I understand why we embraced it. One of the reasons was that, politically speaking, we felt that it was safer. The issues of what men do to women were already bringing the fact of women's political oppression too close to home — literally. Activists could sense it from the start. In attempting to raise consciousness about sexual abuse, we could hear women muttering, "You don't mean all men do you?" Even without the sex factored in, many were reacting as if they knew that our analyses and research were asking them to consider the viability of their heterosexual relationships.

We wound up de-sexualizing the violence issues because we suspected that if we didn't — and we are finding out in the nineties that we were right — that we would trigger what is now known as the sex wars in feminism. The stakes were too high, the women's movement too fragile to shake it up too much.

So, when feminists first took on the issue of rape, for example, and engaged in public education about the subject, we insisted that rape was an act of power, not sex. I have heard this intoned with religious conviction almost everywhere I've travelled and spoken. This, I think, attests to the success of our own education initiatives, so we can be a little self-congratulatory about it — people definitely took in what we were saying. And obviously, speaking as if the issue is power, not sex, kept the door open to many incipient feminists who otherwise would not have walked through to full-blown feminist consciousness.

But something is not ringing true here. I have the feeling that saying rape has nothing to do with sex had everything to do with feminists not wanting to be perceived as anti-sex. For that would make feminism decidedly, well, unsexy.

But if rape is about violence and not sex, why don't attackers just hit women? If rape is about violence, why do attackers — even if they use Coke bottles or broom sticks, instead of their penises — assault women's sexuality? Why, when rapists talk about why they rape, do they say they were out for sex? They don't talk about a deep hatred of women, and if they do, they find the whole subject extremely sexually arousing. Misogyny is very sexy to many men.

It is as if sex has to remain abstract, an ideal, or it can't be talked about and analyzed. This insistence on isolating sexuality and imagining it untrammelled by patriarchal forces has baffled me. I've often wondered why, when we understand how the forces of male domination have appropriated the legal system, the economy, even something as ineffable as spirituality, we fantasize that they have left sexuality out? I think it's important for us to stop worrying about being anti-sex. Let's call ourselves sex-critical and explore the ways sexuality and violence against women have become such close partners. In our early analyses of pornography we said that it wasn't the sex in pornography that we minded it was the violence. But seen for what it is and how it works, pornography winds up being very much about sex, and is, in fact, one of the forces in culture that promote this partnership of sex and violence. Rape myths — that is, scenarios that show women getting sexual pleasure from rape — are among the favourite fictions of pornographers. When they are presented to men in clinical settings, they have been shown to have an enormous influence on male attitudes towards sexuality. The more they see the more likely they are to believe that women really enjoy rape and prefer force in sex.

So why do so many feminists insist that it is not the sex in pornography that bothers them but the violence? Setting aside the fact that most 'just-sex' pornography is made through the brutal subordination of women (the hands-on or economic coercion happens off camera), the truth still has to be faced that violent pornography, the kind in which the brutality is readily apparent, is made specifically to arouse consumers. This means something. And the profits from the industry suggest that pornography and its imitators in mass media have helped to institute the fusion of sex with violence, gendering sexual practice so that it follows the strict scripts for male dominance and female submission.

These issues of sexuality are in the process of transforming our original assumptions about violence against women in the home as well. Our early analyses focussed on the economic issues and the way they influence women's inability to leave an assaultive relationship. We said that economic dependence on a violent spouse kept women living in situations that were dangerous; propaganda for the nuclear family kept women chained to the role of homemaker, leaving them ill-equipped to go out into the work force to fend for themselves; expensive housing made moving out impossible.

We included an analysis of male power that explained how men are permitted to beat up their wives. Aggression, we said, was promoted as part of maleness. Wanting to push women around was an accepted aspect of male behaviour. This began to explain why female high schoolers living with their parents and so not financially dependent on their batterers were already in violent relationships with boyfriends — we said that boys were being boys.

Nobody was ready to say that sex was being sex. Thus none of these analyses were helping us to resolve the painful question of why women who leave violent spouses return to them, or why a woman would leave one violent spouse only to find another one, or why women remain in violent relationships saying expressly that they do not want to leave.

Consider the story of Hedda Nusbaum, the woman who was charged along with her husband for the murder of their six-year-old daughter. Her devotion to her coked-out child-killing husband Joel Steinberg has compelled feminists to reconsider the easy economic answer and to harden the heretofore soft analysis of sex roles. Middle class, with a job in publishing, the Greenwich Village denizen Nusbaum did not fit the mold of the poor, isolated woman, trapped by the ideology that props up the traditional nuclear family. And when she took the stand at Steinberg's trial, she did not break down and recount how she had been victimized and brutalized by a crazed, controlling man. She still loved him, period.

This vexed some feminists who want victimization to be clear cut; they want bad guys and good women, and when real life shows something else they panic. Instead of trying to understand the phenomenon of re-victimization and romance under patriarchy, some feminists have just dumped all over Nusbaum. Susan Brownmiller, an influential American feminist and the author of *Waverly Place*, a fictional account of the Nusbaum/Steinberg relationship, went so far as to say that Nusbaum ought to do time in jail for letting her daughter die. It's easier to engage in wishful thinking that women are active agents and ultimately culpable than to see how the script for Nusbaum's life was written even before she met Steinberg.

For real sexual experience — especially if it takes place in the form of abuse — is a socializing factor as well. Many women have been victimized sexually or physically as children with the result that an abusive spouse winds up making the universe unfold as it always has. Many women know no other way to be with men.

Nusbaum was locked in a classic dominant/submissive pattern. For her, that was what sex, love and romance was. She construed her husband's jealousy and his desire to keep an iron grip on her life as the clearest evidence that he loved her. Many survivors of similar situations describe the same dynamics. They know that what they are experiencing is violence. They do not like it. But they do not consider it abuse. Instead, they interpret it as love gone wrong. When the assaulters feel contrite after the violence and are reduced to tears and, yes, sexual desire, the belief that love is behind it all intensifies. And nurturing, that essential element of the femininity package, then gets distorted in its own ways as caring women commit themselves to easing what they believe is their spouses' pain. They confuse the controlling behaviours behind raging jealousy with love. They wonder why the violence goes on when they have done everything they can to make it better.

The startling and frightening data on re-victimization has come to light in almost all areas of sexual abuse. Diana Russell (in *The Secret Trauma*, New York: Basic Books, 1986) reports "an extraordinarily strong connection between childhood incest and later experiences of sexual assault." According to her data, 66 percent of incest victims were the victims of rape or attempted rape by a non-relative at some time in their lives, compared with 38 percent of women who were raped as adults but were never sexually abused as children. Close to three times as many incest victims as women who were not incest victims reported having been raped in marriage, and in anecdotal evidence from sexual assault centres, counsellors report that they have encountered 'too many' women who have been raped more than once.

Many activists have been uneasy about this data. They want to make sure that people remain aware that any woman, no matter her age or background, can be victimized. They are worried that identifying a population that may be more vulnerable misses the extent to which sexual abuse is something that affects the female gender as a whole. But Russell's data takes both things into account. Thirty-eight percent of women, she says, will experience sexual assault. That is a phenomenal number. But Russell also insists that the statistics on revictimization remain too compelling to ignore. Nevertheless, longtime crisis workers worry that misogynists will interpret these statistics in all the worst ways: any woman who gets it more than once must want it. This is, after all, how many woman-haters interpret women's patterns of returning to abusive spouses or of finding new assaultive partners.

This kind of misogynist thinking is real, but it would be a disaster if this kind of bigotry became an excuse for avoiding hard issues, especially when so much work is beginning to surface that deals with victimization in feminist terms. Russell's work has led the way, and a groundbreaking study of teenaged prostitution by Mimi Silbert and Ayella Pines ("Early Sexual Exploitation as an Influence in Prostitution," *Social Work*, July-August 1983) also sheds some bright light on how re-victimization works.

Of the juvenile prostitutes surveyed by ex-prostitutes at Delancy house in California, 66 percent reported that they had been victims of incest. Through a lengthy interview process, Pines and Silbert were able to uncover how the experience may have constructed the futures of these young women. Having endured what is usually long-term and relentless abuse in their first sexual encounters, these survivors develop a pattern of tolerating abusive relationships, such as with pimps and customers. They have difficulty recognizing dangerous situations when they are in them. Their ability to make sense of what has happened to them makes them retreat into passivity, self-blame and paralysis.

What all this means is that the experiences of abused

women are not likely to fit into our convenient packages. Organized sex workers insist that economic inequality drives women into the sex trade, and not that young women flee abusive fathers to the marginally improved situation of being controlled by a pimp. Shelter workers have ached while they watched women return to their assaultive partners — something less experienced observers react to with outrage. The latter assume that a heavy dose of women-centered support ought to make the difference, when many assaulted women aren't looking for validation from women. It's acceptance from men that counts to them. And to turn their backs on their husbands is to turn their backs on love.

Incest survivors constitute the extreme, though frequent, cases. Child battery, too, can operate as a training ground as it may have for Hedda Nusbaum, whose past suggests a love-less childhood, conditioning a woman into enough self-hate to think herself useless and her husband a god. Steinberg's were the first long-term sexual ministrations she had encountered and she may have assumed that his sexual demands were typical of a loving relationship. The point is that he made her feel sexual, which in the patriarchal system that had defined her desires, spelled victim.

Ordeal (New York: Citadel, 1980), Linda (Lovelace) Marchiano's account of her nightmare as a pornography 'star,' recalls a profoundly depressing scene in which Marchiano watches a tough young woman walk away from Chuck Traynor, the man who kept Marchiano a sexual slave. Marchiano wonders why she didn't follow the lead of the woman who walked away. The fact is that she couldn't. Traynor had known she wouldn't from the start. Victimizers know how to find these kind of women. Traynor could tell from the moment he first met Marchiano, laid up after a car accident, that he was going to be able to control her. Wife beaters know which women suffer more from low self-esteem. They can tell by how they carry themselves, how they walk,

how they lower their eyes, sometimes even from their tone of
voice. They know who will walk out the door at the first sign
of violence and who will be too paralyzed to do so. Child sexual abusers know which children have the seed of self-esteem
to fend off the attacks and which do not. Perpetrators hover
around the schoolyards looking for the kids who are isolated
and vulnerable. They know because many of them themselves
were victims as kids.

Yes, boys are victimized too. But they don't get re-
victimized. More often they become victimizers instead.
(Some might say this is a form of re-victimization, but I don't
think it's useful to say so in a way that makes it seem that per-
petrating and being victimized as adults is the same thing —
it's something like saying men are oppressed, too.) The fact
that abusers have often experienced sexual initiation as sexual
abuse victims has often been overlooked. Only during childhood do males experience the same sexual vulnerability as
females. The fact that girl victims become re-victimized while
boys grow up to become victimizers is a strong testimony to
the influence of the ideology of male dominance and female
submission. That ideology is able to transform the patterns
arising from the same experience.

Coupled with this ideology, early victimization sets up
expectations of more violence and abuse that create experience in a way that is not likely to be easily fixed. They certainly will not be undermined by sermonizing anti-feminists
who think radical feminists invented sexual abuse. And it
won't be undermined even by the caring and commitment
these women may encounter in a visit to the most sensitized
women's shelter. This does not mean that the work going on
in shelters and rape crisis centres isn't essential to women's
survival. It only ought to keep us aware that we have to resist
simple formulations and put experience before theories, no
matter how useful these theories may have been in the past.

Of all our original formulations we were most passionate

about this one thing — women don't like being abused. Were we avoiding something here, too? Many women do respond sexually to being dominated. This should not be that surprising given our social codes for the accepted vocabulary for love and romance. Men conquer, women surrender. The language of sexuality is profoundly hostile. Men 'put, pork and prick' women while the word *fuck* has almost completely lost its sexual resonance, meaning something more like damage instead.

More and more incest counsellors are reporting that the deepest humilation of the incest survivor is her memory of liking it — she liked the attention, she liked feeling special and, most disturbing, she even had an orgasm. Does this make her any less a victim? Does coming take away her pain? She still does not know who to trust. She still experiences sex as betrayal. She still has bruises on her arm.

In whose interests is it that women's sexuality be constructed in this way? Rather than denying the pleasure women get from pain and degradation, I think we should confront women's sexual surrender as the ultimate act of female oppression. For it creates a system of sexual abuse that guarantees that generations are made vulnerable and available to abusers and to the pornographers who profit both sexually and financially from the abuse.

We were right when we thought, ten years ago, that saying these things out loud might pose some risks. Indeed, bringing all this up has brought it all back home. In fact, it wasn't until feminists started talking about the sex issues that the backlash against radical feminism — from women and from within feminism from the likes of Camille Paglia, and her younger cohorts Katie Roiphe and Christina Hoff Sommers — began to take hold. Is it a coincidence that feminism became the F-word precisely at the point we discovered that 50 percent of sexual violence against women takes place at the hands of men we know? Now you hear women, calling themselves feminists, saying young women should learn how to handle a pass at the office, that crying date rape is an excuse for young women not to learn how to negotiate their way through regular encounters and that feminists' obsession with these issues gets in the way of everyday interactions.

Well, I think everyday interactions have to be interrupted and that we need to transform the world in a way so that sexual abuse does not become defined as a part of 'regular' sexual life.

FEELING THE PINCH
ON HARASSMENT

THE PAST IS coming back to haunt a host of politicos and
other public figures and, despite their claims that they are the
victims of a generation gap in sexual values, there is little
indication that the trend is going to stop. I'm talking about
women who are calling men in power on their abusive sexual
behaviour.

Last fall, Ontario judge Walter Hrychuk faced highly
publicized allegations of harassment from two female crown
attorneys, who described the so-called 'kissing judge's' severe
case of wandering hand and lip trouble. His idea of professional conduct included keeping a light fixture in his judge's
chambers designed with a penis as the switch. South of the
border, US Republican senator Robert Packwood is giving
new meaning to the campaign term 'pressing the flesh.' He
faces allegations of sexual harassment from no less than seventeen women who, in the course of their work with the
senator, say they had to cope with unwanted touching and
kissing.

Don't confuse these with Anita Hill/Clarence Thomas
replays. Thomas, as you'll recall, denied everything from the
start. But in both of these cases, the perpetrators — with the
support of their colleagues — think they can wriggle out of

Originally published in *Herizons*, Summer 1994.

the mess by pretending that nothing unusual took place.

Hrychuk painted himself as a jocular, friendly guy who was misunderstood by his hypersensitive female associates. Some of his fellow lawyers and judges went so far as to testify at Hrychuk's hearing that Hrychuk's behaviours were part of the professional package. It's as if they were asking the proceedings to pronounce Hrychuck's behaviour officially normal.

Packwood says simply that he forgets everything — his own twisted way of suggesting that nothing out of the ordinary occurred. In an interview with Barbara Walters, Packwood said he could not remember a single one of the thirty-two incidents. That may have some legal meaning in a court of law, but as a public pronouncement of innocence, it's a dud. The "I see hundreds of women in a given work week" line gives the distinct impression that Packwood routinely sticks his tongue down the throat of any woman he deals with professionally.

Now Paula Jones alleges that US President Bill Clinton made humiliating sexual advances toward her, including dropping his pants in a hotel room, while he was governor of Arkansas in 1991. Some people would say all this started with Donna Rice. She's the woman who had an affair with Gary Hart while he was campaigning to gain the Democratic nomination in the 1988 presidential election. But the Rice case was different. Gary Hart was hounded by a specifically righteous pack who thought outing the candidate as skirt-chaser would impress the moral majority. None of the discussion of his behaviour was framed in terms of women's experience. Donna Rice, as far as I know, never complained about her treatment. And Lee Hart was devastated, but not because she'd just discovered that Gary slept around — for all we know, she may have had what's called an arrangement with her husband, an arrangment that suited her just fine. She was upset because this one fling, now leaked, had sunk the campaign. Michael Dukakis eventually took the nomination, leaving the Bush-league Republicans to sweep the nation.

To this day Clinton supporters insist that tenacious investigations into the president's past financial fiddlings are the result of dirty tricks on the part of the conservative contingent, that Paula Jones is working for the Republicans and that sexual harassment is being used as a weapon by moralists against progressive politicians (check out how Preston Manning wants to monitor the morals of MPs here in Canada). Thirty years ago, I would have said that Kennedy's priapic pursuits were incidental to his ability to lead and today, Jones's naysayers argue that a young woman in a man's hotel room might expect this sort of thing and that Clinton is guilty only of a sloppy seduction attempt.

But today is different. Feminists have redefined the terms. Paula Jones, whether or not she's in the Republican party's pocket, is using very specific language. She felt humiliated, she says. And like the images of Kennedy's between-meeting quickies, arranged by his personal pimps, the secret service, Jones's explicit accounts of Clinton's antics evoke an ultra obnoxious scenario in which a male pol and his buds were deploying their power for sexual gain.

There is no way Hrychuk, Packwood or Clinton could have predicted that any of this would happen to them. Hrychuk thought his behaviour suited the men's club he'd joined. The women confronting Packwood, women who worked for him and consulted with him, didn't amount to enough to trigger even the slightest recollection on his part. Kennedy? The hundreds of women who were sent to the oval office remain nameless. And Clinton: he has to be shaking his head. How could a couple of drinks with a few junior female aides mean a damn thing?

Well, guess what's new in the ninties? Women matter. The rules have changed, and a generation of male professionals had best get used to the collective shock as it continues on its collision course with female consciousness.

INCEST: CONFLICTING INTERESTS

I

IN THE EARLY 1970s, when women gathered in different parts of the country to uncover the prevalence of violence against women, the anger that simmered in these forums was palpable and energizing, so much so that it created a groundswell of activism. Women were naming what was happening to them, giving it a political meaning, identifying the victimization as a crisis. The crimes against women were so numerous, and creating such a collective destruction, that the groundswell turned into a construction of shelters and rape crisis centres. These feminist institutions have redefined the terms 'rape' and 'battery,' have maintained women-centered approaches for assisting women to deal with their crises, and helped survivors generate the resources, both emotional and financial, to cope with the legal system and to get on with their lives in safety.

In the 1980s, the crime commanding the most attention is incest. Its prevalence is greater than even the most sensitive feminist could have imagined, and the damage devastating. Yet there is no similar wave of feminist activists committed to fighting incest, no coalition with the political clout of the Ontario Association of Interval and Transition Houses or the Ontario Coalition of Rape Crisis Centres. Crucially, unlike

From *Broadside*, February 1987.

the situation with rape and assault, the absence of feminist organizing has not created a vacuum in which the sexual abuse is being ignored. On the contrary, an assortment of powerful agencies, social workers, therapists and psychiatrists, most of whom use traditional therapy models, have been deluged with funds for treating the problem. But what they see as the problem and the way to deal with it are different, sometimes diametrically opposed, to the principles and politics feminists bring to the issue.

One of the hardest parts of approaching the issue of incest is digesting the astounding numbers. Diana Russell's survey, conducted in the mid-1980s and discussed in "Sexualizing Violence" in this section, is considered the most reliable because it is the only random survey ever undertaken. In it, she reports that one out of six women will be incestuously assaulted before the age of eighteen, and one out of five will be victimized at some time in her life. Eighteen percent of these assaults were father/daughter incest. The majority of assaults were made by uncles. Eleven percent of the respondents reported that the abuse occurred for the first time before they were five years old. Many women have memories of being assaulted in their cribs. Russell defines incest as "any kind of exploitive sexual contact or attempted contact that hasoccurred between relatives no matter how distant."

When feminists began to talk about rape, we uncovered the fact that sexual assault encompasses more than penile penetration and ejaculation (even though at the time the law addressed only those activities), and Russell has made similar discoveries about incest. She purposely did not restrict her definition of sexual contact to vaginal intercourse, because she learned that there are other areas of the body that are under attack. In fact, the most common area of assault is the mouth because it is the easiest part of the body to get to. It is not clear how many victims' well-meaning but ill-informed therapists have missed the abuse by questioning children about adults who may have touched their 'private' parts.

In other ways, though, Russell's definition is very strict. It does not include what her respondents identified as 'wanted contact,' and this tended to include sibling incest, a form of incest some researchers, David Finkelhor and Janet Meiselman in particular, do not describe as harmful. For Russell though, the issues of how women are trained to submission and to the genuine belief that they have consented to the conditions of their lives are critical ones. But she felt that unless she kept the definition narrow, the credibility of her obviously feminist study would suffer.

Her definition does not include assaults to the eyes and ears: a child who is forced to watch a male relative masturbate is not counted as a victim in Russell's sample. Verbal assaults are not included, nor is a girl or woman who is forced by a relative to look at pornography by itself and with no physical contact considered incestuously victimized in the study. Russell took her sample from 930 random households in San Francisco. Consequently, the relevant data does not include women in institutions (where survivors are reported to be numerous), women on the streets (50 percent of female runaways have run from incest), women who can't remember (many survivors don't) and women who, for whatever reasons, refused to participate in the survey when they were approached.

Russell's numbers are mind-boggling, but given the narrowness of her definition and the relative narrowness of her sample, we have to face the fact that even her astounding numbers are low.

Incest is not a crime of passion or a sudden unplanned assault. According to the reports of many who have counselled perpetrators, the perpetrators of incest strategize intensely, working out the infinitesimal details of the assault, some of them already planning the assault while their wives, sisters-in-law, daughters or nieces are pregnant with the potential victim.

Once the girl is born, perpetrators plot to gain increased access to the child, inundating her with gifts and treats and arranging special outings. The key is to keep the young girl away from her mother and father, or in the case of father/daughter incest, from the mother. Fathers who assault their baby daughters often commit the assault while changing diapers. In the case of older children, the seduction is often carried out to make the girl feel she is involved in a very special relationship, something only she and her new 'friend' can know about and understand. Soon, the child is expected to listen to adult problems as the abuser-to-be begins to share his troubles — how hard it is for him at work, and then how hard it is for him to make friends and be close to people. A father about to assault his daughter inevitably complains that his wife is not 'nice to him,' thus bestowing on his daughter the role of special friend while driving a wedge between the victim and her mother. Soon, 'not nice to him' means not having enough or the right kind of sex with him, and the 'sex education' of his daughter begins. The victim graduates through the education process from being confidante, to being experimentally touched, to being sexually assaulted.

From the beginning, secrecy is introduced. While the child is young, the bargain is less likely to be jeopardized, but as the child grows older and begins to get a sense that there may be something happening that is worth telling someone, the threats from the attacker escalate and often turn violent. In many cases, incestuous fathers keep their victim in line by agreeing not to rape her younger sister, though often they do anyway, and without the older sister knowing. When a victim decides to have a boyfriend, incest offenders grow panicky and more violent. Stepfathers are reported to be the most physically dangerous. Every survivor whom feminist therapist Julie Brickman encountered had done everything she could think of to stop the abuse: begging for a locked bedroom, asking not to be bathed by their incestuous fathers, trying to avoid 'special outings,' pleading to go shopping with their mothers rather than remain with their abusers. And surprisingly, many victims have told somebody about what was happening to them.

According to Russell's survey, a full 17 percent of incest victims told someone at, or close to the time, of the assault and only 5 percent of the victims had never told anybody at any time. Feminists found that, contrary to social conventions, incest was not taboo, but talking about it was. But now we learn that the problem is not necessarily that victims remain silent, but that they are either ignored or not believed.

Generally, the portrait of the abuser is that of a powerful, intrusive and self-serving man, and the portrait of the victim that of an active and resistant girl. But in the vast majority of cases, this resistance fails to end the abuse. Thus "powerlessness," as Julie Brickman says, "is not, for incest victims, a psychological experience."

Some women never escape. Toronto-based counsellors Michele Dore and Wendy Barrett, who co-facilitate a group for adult survivors, talked with one victim who, at age forty-five, was still raped by her father. She is not convinced the abuse will end until her father is dead. Other women develop tactics for self-protection as they grow older. Leaving the family is one strategy. Leaving town is another, in the case of ongoing abuse at the hands of a relative outside the immediate family. Some women leave as a matter of course to go to school, to live on their own or to marry. They often do not show up for family gatherings, and if they must, try and make sure there is someone in the room with them while their abusers are there.

But a survivor who escapes her abuser does not necessarily leave the experience behind. Many of the lingering effects are physical: headaches or sleepless nights that are the vestige of childhood fears that the bedroom door could open at any time. Survivors' relationship to their body is invariably one of ambivalence and mistrust. Many fear getting undressed, others have a feeling of living from the neck up. Often survivors go on to abuse their own bodies. The ambivalence and mistrust extend to survivors' sexuality. Some experience lack of interest in sex; some experience conflict and a difficulty in saying no when they don't want sex; some experience confusion about the meaning of orgasm and the pleasure they felt while being victimized as a child. Incest is also a training ground for emotional patterns and personal identity. Survivors are women who have been profoundly betrayed in relationships they believed were loving and protective. Their sense of reality about relationships in adult life can be distorted. They have difficulty identifying exploitative behaviour and distinguishing between situations that are safe and unsafe. This has created a syndrome identified by feminists as re-victimization. A disproportionate number of rape victims are incest survivors, for example. A study of teenaged prostitutes by Mimi Silbert and Ayella Pines (see "Sexualizing Violence" in this section) revealed that a full two thirds of the juveniles interviewed had been sexually assaulted as children and now were experiencing more violence on the street.

Feminists have been uneasy with this data and are aware that the statistics have to be interpreted with a great deal of care. Saying that women are re-victimized is not the same as blaming the victim. Saying that a high proportion of teenaged prostitutes are incest survivors is not to isolate prostitutes, to create a hierarchy of victimization or to trivialize the prevalence of incest across classes and professions as a political fact of women's lives. Rather, this analysis attempts to make sense out of women's experience, and to understand how sexual abuse trains women to powerlessness. An incest survivor has never really owned her body, and under these circumstances, renting her body will not feel like much of an intrusion. She might also be able to tolerate the particular forms of violence prostitutes experience because she feel as if the universe is unfolding as it always has.

In her keynote address to a sexuality conference in Toronto last fall, Sandra Butler described re-victimization as the difficulty survivors have negotiating their own friends and needs. She went on to say that, in particular, survivors recount experiences that show their trouble identifying violent or dismissive behaviour. Women who feel this way are more likely to be vulnerable to rapists. They will not know when they are safe. They may even be dependent on aggressive men. Male predators, rapists or pimps, know how to find these women. Those men are to blame for the abuse, not the women they have targeted.

II

"If survivors had not spoken," Butler says, "and if feminists had not heard, there would be no work on sexual abuse." But the work on incest, and the so-called treatment administered to survivors has not remained in the hands of feminists. With minimal input from the feminist community, incest remains the purview of the child protection movement, controlled by professionals who practice traditional models of therapy. They, along with the government, give the appearance that incest is being 'handled,' but it turns out that it is being addressed in ways that are inconsistent with feminist perspectives and which sometimes leave women as vulnerable as ever.

The two perspectives, traditional and feminist, often overlap. Certainly many individuals working within, say, Children's Aid and other areas of the child protection movement are well-versed in the feminist literature and research, and often apply feminism as they administer their work loads. Conversely, many feminist therapists have been known to lapse into roles of authority and judgement. But here the two perspectives will be presented as separate and discrete for the sake of clarity. The idea is to define the perspectives, not to stereotype the people working within them.

The best way to identify a feminist perspective on violence against women is to check for the naming of gender. What police and the media call a domestic dispute, feminists call violence against women in the home. What researchers with avoidance mechanism call marital rape, feminists call the raping of wives. And what a psychiatrist might refer to as the aberrant pathology of incest is called by a feminist therapist the normal exercise of male power and sexuality.

Professionals working through traditional models reinforce traditional family values when they adopt what is called the family systems approach to incest therapy. This is the most egregious example of how incest can be politically decontextualized, as therapists set out to treat the 'incestuous family.' According to the values of this treatment, incest is a signal of the family dysfunction in which every family member plays a part. Something has gone wrong in the otherwise safe place of the family home, and through treatment of the entire family, traditional therapists will set it right. Feminists insist that it will never work, that the family has never been a safe place for women and has been the locus of male power, the most concrete expression of which is incest.

"Families don't commit incest, men do," says Wendy Barrett, and consequently feminists have less interest in reconstructing the family than they do in healing whatever can be salvaged of women's lives.

The family systems proponents, when they confront the actual perpetrators, find it hard to blame the offender for the assault. Instead, he is sick, and curable, provided he has the help of a skilled therapist. But while traditional treatments regard the offender as aberrant, feminists refuse to identify the behaviour as part of an individual pathology or as a 'mistake.' Instead they see the behaviour as consistent with other social values, the values conveyed in pornography — *Playboy* doesn't call them Playmates for nothing — or in other mass media that infantilize women, or institutions that glorify male violence and link it to the male sex role. Incest is the inevitable outgrowth of normal sexist sex-role development, part of the institution of compulsory heterosexuality and a key element of women's training to be dependent and attracted to their violators.

Traditional models call for offenders to be treated and families to be reunited. Feminists demand that society be overhauled so that men are not gendered as victimizers and women are not gendered as victims.

As for the male offender, he is a criminal in the feminist view and should be jailed for the assault, even if he is getting treatment of whatever kind. All treatment is experimental. There isn't a single therapist who has been able to say with absolute certainty that if an offender goes through a particular treatment he will not offend again. To date, the safest strategy is incarceration. "No," say some professionals, mustering up sympathy, "these poor fellows are sick and need help. Besides, many of the children don't want their father or their relatives to have to disappear."

Why do we lock up men for stealing property or breaking and entering, sometimes keeping them in jails for years, and coddle child rapists? Why when the break-in is into a child's body do we excuse it? Feminists working in the area of incest have been committed to making perpetrators responsible and nobody else. This view has brought them into conflict with traditionalists who, armed with their family systems theory, find all kinds of ways to turn the offender into a beleaguered and sympathetic character. And there is no better way to generate sympathy for the offenders than to malign the mothers of incest victims. Mothers are blamed for everything and have shouldered the responsibility for their children's delinquent behaviour in other social work models, but the targeting of the mothers of incest offenders is particularly obnoxious. The myths about mothers of father/daughter incest victims are especially vicious. Here they are stated in their classic form by Julie Brickman, one of their staunchest critics: "A cold and rejecting mother initially twists the emotional and sexual development of her boy, which delivers him into the hands of a wife who deprives him of sexual and conjugal rights and finally sets him up for a sexual relationship with his seductive daughter."

Notice how in this scenario the man's actions disappear, and how the perpetrator has become the victim. Here, mothers know their husbands are raping their daughters and still stay silent to protect themselves and their husbands. A recent episode of the TV drama series *Cagney and Lacey*, which usually gets these things right, got it wrong when the script portrayed the mother of an incest victim unsympathetically, showing her withholding evidence from the police and physically assaulting her daughter. If a girl does not know when her own sister is being victimized in the same bedroom, how is a mother supposed to know, especially when the father has actively sought to estrange his daughter from his wife? Whatever relationship existed between a daughter and mother, father/daughter incest ruins it. The degree to which mothers 'collude' is the degree to which they have been rendered powerless. How they lost that power is a matter of conjecture, but it is worth noting the staggering number — 80 percent — of mothers of incest victims (of all kinds, not just father/daughter) who are survivors of incest themselves.

They are not secondary offenders, they are secondary victims. But not according to a great deal of the research contained in a body of literature that has to be read with increasing vigilance. One study describes mothers who ask their husbands to cover up their daughters who are sleeping nude as "setting up situations." The same study assesses women who worked nights as "failing to protect the victim." No wonder a study of Iowa identified the mothers in 65 percent of the cases to be as responsible for father/daughter incest as the fathers. The (American) Center on Child Abuse and Neglect actually lists women 'who fail to protect' as offenders, reporting that a full 46 percent of incest offenders are women, even though the women did not commit the actual offense. Feminists regard these statistics with increasing fury, knowing that if men were not raping their daughters, there would be no reason for this irrational anger to be directed against these women. The key is to bridge the distance, to find some common ground. Male interests often subvert the relationships among women and incest is one of the most effective forms of this kind of sabotage. Trying to rebuild the bond between survivors and their mothers should be a feminist priority.

Another important failure of traditional strategies for treating incest is that they concentrate on children and almost entirely ignore adult survivors. It's been left to feminist therapists to heal the ever-burgeoning population of adult women who are only now prepared to talk about the abuse. Some women are just remembering the trauma after years of keeping the memory locked away and repressed.

Unlike the professional stance of the social worker or the psychiatrist whose relationships to clients tends to fit the 'objective' we/they construction, a feminist approach understands that the distance between counsellor and client is a false one. We are all women, all vulnerable. Most of use have had our relationships with women distorted by our belief that male need was what counted. Most of us have been the victims of male violence. We are all survivors in some way. Women who are incest survivors, or who know of survivors, should be aware that the 'professionals' may not be providing the best care, or that contact with child protection agencies needs to be supplemented by woman-centred input into the trauma of incest. Rape crisis centres often have specific information on incest, and their feminist approach to sexual assault will lead survivors onto the right route. Many women's shelters have begun a special education process on incest and have the knowledge to guide survivors to feminist resources and counsellors.

Perhaps in a few years we will be able to report a burgeoning movement against incest, one that mirrors feminist efforts against rape and wife assault. We need more feminist therapists, more skilled counsellors, the kind that can develop only through a network of survivors and feminists committed to women. This is what government agencies — the Secretary of State Women's Program, the Ontario Women's Directorate, Health and Welfare, Community and Social Services — and other organizations should be funding: feminist conferences on incest, groups for adult survivors and support for a political coalition of incest resisters including survivors, therapists and other feminists making the links between incest and other forms of violence against women.

The need is obvious, close to desperate, for the conditions we are in are very close to those of wartime. There is an eerie similarity between the testimony of incest survivors and the accounts of the survivors of torture. The abusers use the same tactic. "It is as if they all went to the same school," said counsellor Michele Dore, describing the phenomenon. "'You are worthless,' they say, in order to keep us from caring about ourselves. 'You really want this,' they say, to make it impossible for us to believe that we can define our own lives. 'No one will believe you, if you tell,' they say, to keep us silent."

UPDATE 1995

Since "Incest: Conflicting Interests" was published in 1987, a new network of feminist organizing against incest has taken root and the floodgates have opened to the stories of abuse survivors.

But the flow has been directed by two things that have shaped the incest issue like no other issue of violence against women. To begin with, as discussed above, once incest became recognized as the epidemic it is, existing organizations and services falling under the rubric of the child protection movement saw it as their mandate to take action. Feminist activists have had to struggle for their place in the fight against incest, making sure that values centering on preserving the family, and counselling based on family systems models were met with a hard-nosed analysis of the family as the centre of male power and with the bold insistence that perpetrators be made accountable, and not other family members caught in the web of male control.

Second, and eventually even more explosive, the issue of incest and its profound effect on women's psyches led feminists to take therapy seriously as part of the healing process. In many ways this was quite new. Rape crisis centres always distinguished between counselling and therapy. Shelters for assaulted women made a point of recognizing that the job of the shelter worker is to make residents aware of their choices, guide them through the legal system and assist them with getting housing, jobs, government assistance and anything else required to get on with their lives. Pathologizing the women seeking help has historically been seen as inappropriate — the person with the problem was the perpetrator, not the victims. Indeed, any attempt to 'therapize' was seen as unnecessarily invasive — women came to crisis centres for safety, not to be headshrunk, or to be put in situations where past difficulties and traumas were dredged up.

In fact, early feminist thought — evident in the process of consciousness-raising groups as well as in books like Phyllis Chesler's *Women and Madness* — was decidedly hostile to existing systems of therapy. Women are not crazy, we said. Rather, society makes us so. Indeed, we turned traditional formulations around to say that, given the way women are silenced, left with no choices, forced into the home, made to put up with violent men, called hysterical when their emotions became intense, it's a wonder that all women aren't out of our minds by society's terms. Elizabeth Fry Societies (who work with women in conflict with the law in Canada) were discovering that over 90 percent of women in jail had been sexually abused. Jail was just another vehicle for re-victimization. We recognized that what psychiatric institutions and medical minds were doing to women — hitting them up with psychotropic drugs and making them vulnerable to sexual assault in psychiatric hospitals, to use just two examples — constituted new forms of violence against women.

But the experience of incest and its effects on women and on women's institutions in particular forced a change in feminist perceptions. Rape crisis centres were being faced with clients who reported they had been raped not once but fifty times over a period of years and the damage was too devastating and immobilizing to pretend that it didn't exist. Elizabeth Fry Societies were dealing with women so unable to cope in the outside world that they actually yearned for the rigidity of jail and an environment in which they did not have to cope with the overwhelming task of controlling their own lives. Madness could no longer be perceived only as a sane response to a world of male power. Rather, feminists have come to realize that psychic trauma is, in and of itself, the stuff of women's oppression.

Healing a wounded community became a priority — using therapies, yes, but with a difference. The therapist was not god pronouncing on mental health. She was a woman like her client. She did not pathologize the woman who came to her — calling her experience a syndrome or her pain a disease — but, together with survivor activists, and as survivors themselves, stayed true to the view that the lives of survivors were shaped by their early trauma and that their behaviours, under the circumstances, made absolute sense. It was women's

stories of incest that led feminist therapists to new perspectives on traditional psychiatric diagnoses. What psychiatrists
called borderline and histrionic personalities, feminists called
the multiple personalities and dissociative strategies necessary
for victims' survival. Self-help was seen as an empowering
strategy. The sense of connectedness to other survivors, discovered to be so important at rape speakouts and safe havens,
was nurtured in survivor groups.

Not everyone has been happy with the new developments. Even some of the strongest anti-incest advocates
remain leery of the new therapy oriented bent of the anti-
incest movement. Louise Armstrong, author of *Kiss Daddy
Goodnight* (New York: Hawthorne, 1978) says in her newest
book, *Rocking the Cradle of Sexual Politics* (Reading: Addison
Wesley, 1994) that radical feminist politics are losing their
edge as women get caught up in their twelve-step programs.
She says we are abandoning the political work that kept the
meaning of male power front and centre in the discussion
and ensured that perpetrators were charged and convicted.

I think this is another of those complex issues where two
things can be true at the same time. Yes, education about
incest has to be education about male power, and perpetrators should be made responsible for their crimes. But those
things can't happen without political work and I think a
healed survivor makes for a more effective political activist.

Indeed, women speaking of their experiences along with
survivor group activism *have* helped to shift the social and
political ground dramatically. When the statute of limitations
— prohibiting court actions against perpetrators over five
years past the crime — was lifted by a Canadian Supreme
Court Ruling in 1992, survivors got the chance to sue their
abusers and the stakes rose up. Perpetrators became seriously
threatened. The anti-incest movement came under full attack.

Leading the charge is the False Memory Syndrome
Foundation (FMSF), the brainchild of Pamela and Peter

Freyd. The couple formed the foundation in Philadelphia in 1992 after they were confronted by their son-in-law about Peter's sexual abuse of their daughter. The Freyds claim that memories of abuse were implanted by their daughter's therapist. Warning that unscrupulous therapists were on the way to exposing innocent parents to public pillory and destroying families in the process, the Freyds welcomed other 'falsely accused' parents into the fold. To date, the foundation claims to have 5,000 such members. It does nothing to screen its members. They are falsely accused only to the extent that they say they are.

Perhaps we should have seen all this coming. Incest has now become instant fodder for the next TV Movie of the Week, public figures like Roseanne and Oprah Winfrey have disclosed as survivors and literary figures as prestigious as Canada's Sylvia Fraser have written openly and honestly about their trauma. Indeed, stories of incest are now so common that a Toronto literary critic recently complained that incest was being used artificially as a literary device. I say to him: stop men from abusing women and women will stop writing about it.

The critic in this case is typical of the ignorant resistance to the facts about incest and its prevalence. "It can't be true," people want to say. The FMSF plays on this collective incredulity, hoping that the public will continue to believe that the numbers of incest reports are just so damned high that all the stories can't possibly be true. The fact that so many incest survivors were recovering memories previously lost left them even more vulnerable to attack. How could anyone forget such a thing? people want to know. In this kind of environment, and given that children who are saying it is happening to them at the actual time of the abuse aren't being believed by the caretakers around them, would anyone believe someone who says it happened over twenty years ago? And who gave her all these ideas in the first place?

Why are therapists implanting these ideas? It must be those feminists making it up, the FMSF answers. This has been a tired refrain from both reactionary right-wing groups and even occasionally now from the new neo-feminists — that feminists invented violence against women as a make-work project so that they can have jobs in shelters and rape crisis centres. Feminists make it up so they can show the universe unfolding according to their paranoid visions. Feminists and feminist therapists turn women into victims when, in truth, they were really cared for and nourished in loving families. These claims go a long way towards making feminist therapists look like the abusers and FMSF look like women's protectors.

The new strategy — targeting the therapist principally and not the survivor — coincides with radical feminists' embrace of healing values. The influence of feminist activists is having a growing influence on women entering therapy. FMSF advocates know this and are fighting it. Getting other psychiatrists on side is part of the strategy, so it's no coincidence that the groundbreaking guide *The Courage to Heal,* by Ellen Bass and Laura Darin, is on the FMSF hit list. *The Courage To Heal* promotes self-help values and women's independence from the psychiatric establishment and the FMSF is doing whatever it can to pit the book, its authors and the movement from which they sprang against psychiatrists and their traditional strategies.

But though feminism and feminist therapy has come under attack, the FMSF is not necessarily leaving survivors alone. Indeed, the story of the head honchos, the Freyds themselves, says alot about FMSF tactics. A paper by the Freyds' daughter Jennifer Freyd, a psychologist at the University of Oregon, and active in the area of memory and trauma, tells the truth about what happened, not about the sexual abuse itself — Jennifer Freyd is clear on her right not to discuss those details publicly — but about how the FMSF has played a role in her re-victimization.

Though the Freyds warn of hysterical women, moved by over-enthusiastic therapists exposing innocent parents to embarassing public scrutiny, it was Pamela and Peter Freyd who invaded Jennifer Freyd's privacy. Pamela wrote about her daughter's so-called false accusations of child sexual abuse and the subsequent effects on the family and distributed the paper widely. Though she wrote the article as Jane Doe, subsequent FMSF newsletters identified Jane Doe as Pamela Freyd, and thus Jennifer as the one with the false memories. According to Jennifer, the Freyds sent the paper to her colleagues during her promotion year at the University of Oregon in an attempt to harass her and undermine her professional credibility. So far, they have been unsuccessful. Crucially, this public campaign against Jennifer took place despite the fact that, until she wrote her 1993 paper, Jennifer *had made no public disclosures of her memories and had not sought charges against her father.*

Though the foundation was plainly formed by the Freyds as a personal weapon, their campaign has been successful enough politically to have left the vague impression on the public consciousness that a False Memory Syndrome exists. It is not, and is not close to being, recognized as such by the American Psychiatric Foundation and even FMSF board members can't agree on what the symptoms of this syndrome might be. Nevertheless, the FMSF keeps trying to shroud itself in a cloak of scientific respectability, taking their show onto the academic hustings. The centrepiece of the research they say proves that all recovered memories are false is a study undertaken by Elizabeth Loftus and her associates. In it, she says she was able to convince a significant sample in her control group that they had been lost in a shopping mall when in fact thay had not. In her report Loftus sees fit to compare getting lost in a shopping centre with severe trauma — a dubious claim — while at the same time stating baldly that there is no evidence to support the fact that memories can be repressed in the first place.

This is categorically not so, but it does play on the public's already fragile sense of the survivors' credibility and on their sense that vulnerable women can be manipulated and made to think they were abused. FMSF advocates claim that memories can't be recovered, only implanted and even wonder how women could forget such events in the first place. New research on memory and how it works, especially by Bessel van der Kolk and Lenore Terr (see further reading below) suggests that there are two memory systems — explicit or declarative memory and implicit, sensorimotor memory. While the explicit or declarative memory that initially records the proper sequence of events may change, the physical and psychological experience of trauma — thanks to various neurochemical processes — imprints itself on the sensorimotor memory. This is the implicit memory and its imprint of the trauma of the event is not lost — it is stored in the body for the person's entire life. Or as van der Kolk puts it, the body keeps the score. The declarative memory, on the other hand, is repressed, buried in the subconscious so deeply that it is forgotten.

But do people actually forget such a devastating experience? In her intriguing research, Linda Myer Williams used as the basis of her work a 1970s study by the National Institute of Mental Health of 213 young women and children who had reported child sexual abuse at the time. Williams involved 129 of the original 213 victims in a questionnaire designed to determine whether the women recalled the abuse. Over 38 percent of her sample did not report the abuse on the questionnaire, though they did disclose other experiences about themselves — experiences such as abortion, prostitution, contracting sexually transmitted diseases, which are stigmatized in society. And contrary to the FMSF claims that women are easily made to believe they have been abused when they have not, many of the subjects appeared truly not to recall the abuse *even when told by the researchers.*

Forgetting, says Jennifer Freyd, is a survival tactic. In her paper she offers a compelling example of how this process operates. Imagine, she says, two people hiking in the bush. One of the hikers trips and breaks her leg. She is in excruciating agony. Unable to move, she lies crumpled on the ground and sends her partner off to find help. Now imagine another hiker trekking on her own. She trips and incurs the same multiple fracture that immobilized the previous hiker. But this woman does not remain motionless on the ground. She stands up and finds a way to get herself to someone who can help. Is she in pain? Yes. What makes her different from the woman who could not move after sustaining the same injuries? Her survival depended on burying her physical pain.

It's hard to assess whether the media needed a False Memory Syndrom Foundation for motivation to subvert the incest movement or whether they would have gotten around to a backlash regardless. The media feeds on the tidbits from the FMSF, not just because it's good sport to lash out at feminist ideas in particular — though it may be — but because the newsdesk needs controversy and thrives on finding the exception. After society's collective surge in consciousness about incest, it was inevitable that newshounds would surround like vultures any whiff of controversy regarding the credibility of survivors.

New York magazine, covering the Imgram case in which it was the abuser who recanted, stated that the prosecution's case was clouded by theories of repressed memories. *Harper's* magazine, reporting on the case against Margaret Kelly Michaels, compared the growing population of survivors confronting their tormenters personally or in the courts years after the abuse with the Salem witch hunts and the excesses of the McCarthy era. And newspapers everywhere had a field day with the case of the McMartin family, charged on 323 indictments of abuse in Manhattan Beach California and later acquitted. The acquittals were based on what was perceived as

overly aggressive interviewing techniques used on the children
by the Children's Institute International. Though newspapers
were quick to say the McMartins had been falsely accused,
there is no reason to conclude from the case that those
charged had not committed the crimes, only that the inves-
tigative techniques were problematic.

Still, the first *Toronto Star* reports on so-called false memory came in the form of a three-part series totalling close to
200 inches of column space. Despite the extraordinary length
of the pieces, they uncovered only one case of so-called false
memory and in that case, the survivor had indeed been
abused, but got the identity of the perpetrator wrong.
Imagine how our newspapers would be dominated by stories
of child sexual abuse, if every case of incest were covered as
thoroughly as these rare cases of alleged false accusations.

The fall-out from the FMSF and the media's submission to
their point of view is already having an effect in the courts. In
June 1994, the accused in *R. v. Baker* was acquitted based on
the claim that therapists at St. Boniface hospital had implanted the memories.

And the FMSF's political attack continues. In the *Toronto
Star,* November 1993, Peter Freyd wrote a letter boasting that
he would succeed in convincing the American Psychiatric
Association to issue an official statement warning against the
misapplication of memory enhancing techniques such as hyp-
nosis, sodium amytal, body massage and *participation in survivor groups* (italics mine). It is dangerous, says Freyd, for
women to meet and speak together about our experiences.

Women telling it as it happened *are* dangerous — to perpetrators and to the institutions that promote abusers' rights
to continue the assaults. It's ironic that the FMSF compares
survivors' searching out their abusers with a massive witch
hunt, when in fact, it's the other way around. The FMSF and
its cronies, and the rest of the forces engaged in the backlash,
are undertaking a modern witch hunt aimed at attacking

women's right to our bodily integrity. It is a common reaction to women's power. Throughout history, whenever women have gathered to share our truths, to challenge accepted sexual practice or to heal ourselves, we have encountered intense persecution.

We are at such a moment in time. Pornography encodes the practice of male power over women inside our bodies. Violence against women and children keeps us in our place — on the bottom, both socially and sexually. Some people desperately want us to stay there. It is precisely because we are forging new ways to express our sexuality, precisely because of the strength we come to possess through recovery, precisely because the power surge in women's resistance has the potential to send the systems of male power crashing into oblivion, that the backlash has become so intense. We are scaring people — and that's a good thing.

This is no time for retreat. As it is, sexual abuse survivors themselves are very susceptible to FMSF propaganda, which is fueling doubts and causing women to question their own recall. There is a fear that women will stop coming forward or stop seeking professional help. Feminist therapists and counsellors, too, have to resist self-doubt and continue to be confident in our original formulations, even as we strive to develop and improve our counselling methods. We cannot allow the backlash to erase the record. Now more than ever, women have to tell their stories and we as feminists have to remain consistent in the strategy of believing them.

If we don't, who will?

FURTHER READING

Ellen Bass and Laura Darin. *The Courage to Heal.* New York: Harper and Row, 1988.

Sven Ake Christianson and Lars-Gören Nilsson. "Hysterical Amnesia: A Case of Aversively Motivated Isolation of Memory." In Trevor Archer and Lars-Gören Nilsson, eds., *Aversion, Avoidance and Anxiety.* Hillside, NJ: Laurence Erlbaum Associates, 1989.

Mary Lou Fassel. "Fighting the False Memory Backlash." Paper presented at the Truth Tellers Conference, Toronto, November 1995.

Jennifer A Freyd. "Theoretical and Personal Perspectives on the Delayed Memory Debate." Paper presented at the Continuing Education Conference, Foote Hospital, Ann Arbor, Michigan, 1993.

J.L. Herman. *Trauma and Recovery.* New York: Basic Books, 1992.

J.L. Herman and E. Schatzow. "Recovery and Verification of Memories of Childhood Sexual Trauma," *Psychoanalytic Psychology* 4 (1987), pp. 1-14.

Wendy Hovdestad and Connie Kristiansen. "Mind Meets Body: On the Nature of Recovered Memories of Trauma." In M. Janic Gutfreund and Susan Contralto, eds., *Women and Therapy,* forthcoming.

Connie Kristenson, Kathleen A. Pelton and Wendy Hovdestad. "Recovered Memories of Child Abuse: Fact, Fantasy or Fancy?" In M. Janic Gutfreund and Susan Contralto, eds., *Women and Therapy,* forthcoming.

Bessel A.Van der Kolk. "The Body Keeps the Score: Memory and the Evolving Psychobiology of Post-traumatic Stress," *Harvard Review of Psychiatry* (Jan/Feb. 1994), pp. 253-265.

Linda Myer Williams. "Recall of Childhood Trauma: A Retrospective Study of Women's Memories and Child Abuse." Paper presented at the Annual Meeting of the American Society of Criminology, 1993.

OTHER BOOKS FROM SECOND STORY PRESS

ADOPTION REUNIONS *McColm*

AS FOR THE SKY, FALLING: A Critical Look at Psychiatry and Suffering *Supeene*

AURAT DURBAR: Writings by Woman of South Asian Origin *Rafiq*

THE BEST LAID PLANS *Ross*

BEYOND HOPE *Zaremba*

THE BIG CARROT VEGETARIAN COOKBOOK *Lukin*

THE BUTTERFLY EFFECT *Zaremba*

CANADIAN FEMINISM AND THE LAW *Razack*

CAST A LONG SHADOW *Lander*

COLLABORATION IN THE FEMININE *Godard*

CONSUMING PASSIONS: Feminist Approaches to Weight
Preoccupations and Eating Disorders *Brown & Jasper*

FACES OF FEMINISM *Harris*

THE FARM & CITY COOKBOOK *McDonald & Morgan*

FOUND TREASURES: Stories by Yiddish Women Writers *Forman, Raicus, Swartz & Wolfe*

FRICTIONS: Stories by Women *Tregebov*

FRICTIONS II: Stories by Women *Tregebov*

INFERTILITY: Old Myths, New Meanings *Rehner*

IN THE NAME OF THE FATHERS: The Story Behind Child Custody *Crean*

THE JOURNAL PROJECT: Dialogues and Conversations Inside
Women's Studies *Putnam, Kidd, Dornan & Moore*

KID CULTURE *McDonnell*

LEGAL TENDER *Foster*

MARGARET ATWOOD'S POWER *Hengen*

MENOPAUSE: A Well Woman Book *Montreal Health Press*

THE MIDDLE CHILDREN *Jacobs*

THE NEW INTERNATIONALIST FOOD BOOK *Wells*

OF CUSTOMS AND EXCISE *Mara*

ON THE ROAD TO VEGETARIAN COOKING *Lukin*

ORGANIZING UNIONS *Cornish & Spink*

OUR LIVES: Lesbian Personal Writings *Rooney*

A PARTISAN'S MEMOIR: Woman of the Holocaust *Schulman*

PORNOGRAPHY AND THE SEX CRISIS *Cole*

POSITIVE WOMEN: Voices of Women Living with AIDS *Rudd & Taylor*

SEXUAL HARASSMENT *Larkin*

SUDDEN MIRACLES: Eight Women Poets *Tregebov*

SUPERWOMEN AND THE DOUBLE BURDEN: Women's Experience of Change
in Central and Eastern Europe and the former Soviet Union *Corrin*

A TASTE FOR JUSTICE COOKBOOK *Bridgehead*

TWIST AND SHOUT: A Decade of Feminist Writing in THIS MAGAZINE *Crean*

UNEASY LIES *Zaremba*

WHAT YOU SEE: Drawings by Gail Geltner

WORK FOR A MILLION *Zaremba*

THE WORLD IN YOUR KITCHEN *Wells*

THE Y CHROMOSOME *Gom*